China and the Credit Crisis

The Emergence of a New World Order

China and the Credit Crisis

The Emergence of a New World Order

Giles Chance

WILEY

John Wiley & Sons (Asia) Pte. Ltd.

Other Wiley Editorial Offices
John Wiley & Sons, Inc., 111 River Street, Hoboken, NJ 07030, USA
John Wiley & Sons, Ltd., The Atrium, Southern Gate, Chichester,
    West Sussex P019 8SQ, UK
John Wiley & Sons (Canada), Ltd., 5353 Dundas Street West, Suite 400,
    Toronto,Ontario M9B 6H8, Canada
JohnWiley & Sons Australia Ltd., 42 McDougall Street, Milton, Queensland 4064,
    Australia
Wiley-VCH, Boschstrasse 12, D-69469 Weinheim, Germany

Library of Congress Cataloging-in-Publication Data
ISBN: 978-0470-82507-5

Typeset in 11.5/14pt Bembo by Laserwords Private Limited, Chennai, India.
Printed in Singapore by Saik Wah Press Pte. Ltd.
10 9 8 7 6 5 4 3 2

This book is dedicated to
Ying, Lao Ye, Lao Lao, Leonora, and Miranda

Contents

Foreword

W hat role did China play in generating the current global financial crisis? In this book, Giles Chance argues that China did not cause the crisis; but without China, the crisis would not have happened. I think his argument is right. The integration of China into the global economy has fundamentally changed the global market structure and financial order. Nevertheless, China's impact has not been well understood and appreciated by academia and policymakers worldwide. In some sense, it is this ignorance of China's new role that misled both the American and the Chinese policymakers in setting their macroeconomic policies, particularly monetary policies, which in turn caused global imbalance and the financial crisis. Now it is time to have a right idea of China and the global economy.

I have known Giles Chance for over 20 years, since I met him when I was completing my doctorate at Oxford University in England. Giles has written his book *China and the Credit Crisis: The Emergence of a New World Order* at a good time. China stands at the entrance to a new era. As Giles suggests, the credit crisis has changed the balance of global financial power. This has altered, and in some ways strengthened,

China's global position. Giles analyzes this new situation in his book, which I think is the first one to cover this subject directly and in some depth. The issues he discusses are all important: China's role in the credit crisis; the effect of the crisis on China; the future role of the dollar; and the consequences of the crisis for China's relations with the United States, Asia, and the emerging world.

This new era will require yet more change within China. China has to shift its growth model away from exports towards a more balanced demand structure, and has to make more productive use of its pool of savings. This structural change requires further reform, for instance in the area of capital markets. To achieve the best results, the role of the market in developing China's economy needs to be continually strengthened. In addition, China's world role is set to become more significant, as the Sino–American relationship deepens and expands, and China starts to play a more active role in global multilateral institutions and world diplomacy.

Giles is the right person to write this book. He has become very familiar with China and its people over more than two decades. His work has involved a wide range of Chinese and foreign companies and institutions. He has taught several classes at the Guanghua School since 1999, and is now a visiting professor at the School. I recommend this important book to people around the world who want to understand better China's emergence as a superpower.

Professor Zhang Wei Ying
Dean, Guanghua School of Management,
Peking University

C hina is playing a crucial role in helping to steer the world out of its worst recession since the era of the Great Depression. Of course, part of the resilience its economy has shown in early 2009 derives from a strenuous, government-led pump-priming exercise. This is interesting but not new; we have all become familiar with China's ability to create muscle-bound expansion. What is fascinating and potentially highly significant about the past few months of China's development is that alongside the self-injected vigor of the RMB 4 trillion state fiscal stimulus program, there are clear signs of self-generating economic activity. In other words, China—robbed of its export engines as global demand collapsed—is starting to run on its own steam, starting to derive the impetus for growth from an inner dynamism and starting to evolve into a continental economy just as the US did in the nineteenth century. Even more intriguing, perhaps, is that the most buoyant parts of the economy since the crisis hit have not been the huge river delta conurbations around places such as Shanghai and Guangzhou but hundreds of smaller, inland cities where people have carried on spending pretty much as if nothing untoward had happened.

The emergence of China as a more self-sustaining continental economy is one of the unexpected by-products of the global economic crisis. There are others too. This year, for the first time in decades, the inflow of foreign direct investment may be outpaced by the outflow of Chinese investment overseas. As the process of overseas acquisitions of companies, brands, technology, and resources continues, China will remodel itself in fundamental ways. Its already rapid climb up the technology ladder will quicken, the brand equity owned by its companies will rise from a currently low level, and its ownership of resources around the world will grow. All of this will propel an ascent up the value chain, but whether this rise will be quick enough to offset several detracting factors is a question that will do much to determine the future trajectory of China's economic development. Among these detractors is the aging population; after 2015, the populace is set to start aging at a rapid rate, increasing the number dependent on the working population year after year. Another frailty is the environment. The cost of clearing up poisoned lakes and rivers, halting the southward march of northern deserts, combating air pollution and addressing the environmental warming that threatens to melt the Himalayan glaciers that feed the headwaters of the Yellow and Yangtze rivers could be forbidding. Whether these and other detractors will come to dominate China's future and that of its interaction with the outside world are crucial questions of our time.

In this clear-eyed and thoughtful book, Giles Chance, who has lived and worked in China for much of the past two decades, delivers a penetrating portrait of China at this crucial juncture in its history. What makes the book particularly valuable is the way it traces internal issues toward their international context. We learn how China's emergence will shake up the existing world order, how the world's most populous nation is set to lead Asia economically and diplomatically, and how wealth and influence will shift from the West to the East. History is usually something that we see clearly only in retrospect, but China is moving so rapidly that with keen observation—such as that supplied in this book—we can get the sense of capturing the historical process in flight.

James Kynge
Editor, FT China Confidential
Author, China Shakes the World

Preface

My unusual experiences in China and with the Chinese over two decades led me to think some years ago about setting down some Chinese thoughts on paper. The catalysts to this book were provided by the credit crisis and its aftermath, and a period of enforced inactivity, with no telephones or family to disturb, in hospital in Kufstein, Austria in December 2008 with a broken leg. A period of two months spent in the French countryside in springtime has enabled me to complete this book about China and its new place in the world. A word or two of background is needed.

Since 1988 China has played a central role in my life and in my professional career. From knowing nothing about the country 20 years ago, my work over two decades has led me into an appreciation of the richness and depth of China's society. Over time, I have become deeply interested in China, both for itself and for its connection with the rest of the world. My first personal contact with China was at the World Bank in Washington DC, where I met one of the first mainland Chinese economists to work there. Nearly four years later, we married in London. Our three-week honeymoon in China became my introduction to this remarkable and vast country. After my first day or two in Beijing, I felt as if I had arrived on a different planet, a sister to the planet Earth, with its own language and culture, its own attitudes, its own way of doing everything, owing virtually nothing to Western civilization. Although no one then was rich in China, at least in a monetary sense, and Chinese infrastructure was often basic, quickly I became aware of deeply ingrained habits of civilization which indicated a country that must once have been dominant and wealthy. Under the mask of adherence to Marxism could be perceived a system which I later understood to be Confucianism, characterized by discipline, practicality, humor, and a strong interest in the outside world.

It seemed to me then that if the Chinese were successful in making their country a better place, China might not be a bad place for an Englishman with a Chinese wife to spend some of his time. Back in London, I changed my career from fund management to Chinese entrepreneur, and started, with my wife, an advisory business aimed at multinationals and Western sources of technology, based in Beijing, Shanghai, and London. This involved me at a basic level in Chinese commercial life in a wide range of industrial sectors, ranging from mobile telephony, naval submarine communications, and aerospace to the automotive industry, commercial banking, real estate, and retail. Later, we founded a securities business which brought Chinese companies to raise capital in London. On many occasions my work has required me to see both sides of a deal. I often heard what the Chinese thought of foreigners, and what foreigners thought of the Chinese. I lived in both Beijing and Shanghai for several years, once in the mid-1990s and again in the early part of the millennium. I rely on this testing and fascinating 20-year journey for my insights into how China thinks and works.

Since the Second World War, the global leadership of the United States has been unquestioned, thanks to the dollar's role as the world currency, the size of America's financial markets and economy, and the reach of American military power. I would like my American readers to understand that, when I consider the causes of the financial crisis, it is for this reason of global dominance that American policymakers receive a disproportionate amount of attention in this book. I am not anti-American; in fact, quite the opposite. As a Fulbright scholar, I feel I owe Senator Fulbright a debt, and my time at the Tuck business school at Dartmouth College and working in America gave me great admiration for the American spirit and way of life.

In writing *China and the Credit Crisis*, I have addressed the well-informed general reader, who wants to explore important current trends and understand them better. I have tried to write the book to be readable and digestible, but without misrepresenting or omitting important economic or financial issues. The book is not aimed at China specialists or at professional economists, who will be familiar with much of the history and argument which is set out here as a necessary background for the less well-prepared reader. Nevertheless, I hope that representatives from both of these tribes of specialists may find ideas in the book which suggest further research.

I was very happy when the Singapore office of John Wiley & Sons showed an interest in my book proposal. I could not have asked for a better publisher to work with. My thanks go to CJ Hwu, Nick Wallwork, and the team at Wiley, and also to James Kynge of the *Financial Times* for making the introduction. I have been fortunate to have had assistance and support from a number of well-qualified people. I am grateful to Professor Zhang Wei Ying, dean of the Guanghua School of Management at Peking University, and to James Kynge of the *Financial Times* for their advice, and for writing excellent forewords to the book. Glenn Buckles, Jonathan Hall, Nancy Stewart, Richard Camhi, Irene Noel, and Andrew Ballingal read all of, or substantial amounts of, the text. I thank them all for their kind and helpful assistance, corrections, and encouragement. The attention paid in the book to the issue of Chinese savings is due to Professor Robert Neild, Fellow of Trinity College, Cambridge, who alerted me to this issue. He also kindly read through Chapter 2 and provided important encouragement, as did another Fellow of Trinity College, Cambridge, Professor Sir James Mirrlees. David Cobbold gave me suggestions on the Chinese currency and on the euro which led directly to discussions in Chapters 2 and 5. I owe Geoffrey Barker, of Ballingal Investment Advisors, credit for much of the conceptual background to Chapter 2 and other ideas besides. Dr. Linda Goldberg at the Federal Reserve in New York provided useful economic background and encouragement. Thanks to Richard McGregor of the *Financial Times* for sharing some of his insights into the current and future China scene. Arun Singh OBE provided me with a fascinating Indian perspective on the Sino–Indian relationship. Hugh Trenchard and Dr. John Villiers gave me essential perspectives on Japan's relationship with China from their deep knowledge of the country. Thanks also to Toby Beaufoy, David Lorimer, and my cousin Toby Chance for their encouragement and advice, and to William Beaufoy for his comments. I am grateful to Aron Buckles for permission to read and refer to his Masters thesis.

In particular, though, I am grateful to my wife Ying for her wise advice, criticism, and great support, and to my family for their amused tolerance during the project. I dedicate this book to them.

Giles Chance
Guanghua School of Management, Peking University
October 2009

1

The World has Changed

In the spring of 1999 I was teaching 54 Chinese graduate students at the Peking University business school in Beijing. Against the background of the NATO bombing of Serbia, on Friday May 7 a NATO aircraft bombed and destroyed the Chinese consulate in Belgrade, killing three Chinese nationals. The Chinese suspected the bombing was deliberate, and immediately complained strongly to the United States. My next class fell in the morning of the following day. Only a handful of students showed up. The rest were demonstrating outside the United States Embassy in Beijing. They stayed there for nearly a week, hurling stones through the Embassy windows, while the Ambassador James Sasser sat inside.

It now seems highly likely that the NATO bombing of the Chinese consulate was deliberate, and it appears that NATO felt itself not only justified but safe in taking a highly aggressive action against Chinese interests, extending even to loss of Chinese life. In October 1999 a report in a British newspaper[1] confirmed that NATO had deliberately bombed the Chinese consulate in Belgrade, after discovering that the building was being used to rebroadcast Serbian army communications. According to senior military and intelligence sources in Europe and the United States, the Chinese embassy was removed from a list of prohibited targets after NATO electronic intelligence detected the emanation from the embassy of military messages to Milosevic's forces. The story at the time, that NATO had confused the coordinates of the consulate's locations, appears to have been a fabrication.

At the end of May 1999, an article written by Stephen Yates, an analyst at the conservative US think-tank The Heritage Foundation, illustrated how conservative American sentiment stood towards China at the time. It commented:

Although the bombing [of the Chinese consulate] was a tragedy, the United States should not overreact to China's stage-managed protests. These protests call into question the overly optimistic objective of establishing a "constructive strategic partnership" with China. The US relationship with China needs to be placed on firmer ground with more realistic expectations and a greater appreciation of US long-range interests in Asia.[2]

Two years later, in April 2001, a US surveillance plane monitoring China's coastline collided with one of two Chinese J-8 fighters that had been shadowing it, killing the Chinese pilot and forcing the US aircraft to make an emergency landing on Hainan Island, at the southernmost point of China's mainland.[3] Although the US aircraft was apparently operating just outside Chinese airspace, the incident was only resolved, and the aircraft's 24 crew released, after President George W Bush had written a letter to his opposite number, President Jiang Zemin, apologizing for the incident.

A Permanent Shift of Power and Influence

China's position in the world has changed dramatically since 2001, and it will go on changing. This book is about a permanent shift of economic power and influence towards Asia, in particular towards China. Nearly eight years after the Hainan incident, in February 2009, Hillary Clinton, recently sworn in as the new US Secretary of State, made her first overseas visit. Not to Canada, or to Europe, but to Asia. This made her the first new Secretary of State since Dean Acheson, nearly 60 years before, to start an inaugural overseas trip in a westerly, rather than easterly or northerly, direction. With Tokyo, Seoul, and Beijing on her itinerary, she left China till last. In deference to the long-standing US alliances with Japan and South Korea, she could not have visited Beijing first.

But there was no doubt that the China leg of her visit was the most important. A contemporary editorial commenting on the trip, which appeared in *The Times* of London, stated:

On almost every global issue, China's policies are crucial. A Chinese veto on sanctions against Sudan or Zimbabwe sabotages hopes for tougher United Nations action on Darfur or Robert Mugabe. As the world's third largest economy and largest carbon emitter, China holds the key on climate change. On energy security, nuclear proliferation in Iran and North Korea or the junta in Burma, no co-ordinated action is possible without China.[4]

Hillary Clinton's public address in Beijing reflected these realities. "The opportunities for us to work together are unmatched anywhere in the world," she said in her speech.[5] At their first meeting on the edge of the G20 London summit in April 2009, Presidents Hu Jintao and Barack Obama followed up Hillary Clinton's visit with an agreement for the US and China to hold a strategic and economic dialogue, to be led by the President's most senior lieutenants—Secretary of State Hillary Clinton and Treasury Secretary Tim Geithner. The dialogue would be based on the bilateral discussions covering economic and trade matters which had been set up by George W Bush in 2006. However, in President Obama's words, the US–China dialogue would be broadened out to "help set the stage for how the world deals with a whole host of challenges,"[6] signaling a significant upgrading and extending of the US relationship with China. President Hu's comment on the initiative was equally positive, but carried a subtly different message:

> *Good relations with the United States are not only in the interest of the two peoples, but also beneficial to the peace, stability and prosperity of the Asia–Pacific region, and the world at large.*[7]

Even at this early stage in the new American President's term, Hu wanted to highlight China's relationship with the United States as a key link between the rich world and poorer, developing countries—a link which only China, itself a developing country, could make, and an important source of China's future global influence.

The tectonic plates which underlie the global architecture of power and influence started shifting some time ago. The premise of this book is that the global financial crisis was a major tremor which accelerated this global shift in power and influence, away from the developed world led by the US, towards Asia and the developing world. This book's purpose is to show how China's emergence contributed to the crisis, and as far as it is possible to tell at this early stage, what some of the major consequences of the shift could be for key aspects of international relations, and for the Chinese themselves. When we hear the President of Brazil, Luiz Inacio Lula da Silva, blaming the financial crisis on "white people with blue eyes," we know that already we are traveling through landscape that we in developed Western countries may not recognize.[8] The need to take stock of where we are going has become pressing. Soon the landscape passing outside our window will become strange and unfamiliar. This book is intended to help us give some thought to where we are headed.

The China Effect

Part of the story of China and the credit crisis concerns China's involvement with the economic conditions underlying the crisis. The crisis occurred because of too much debt, which appeared cheap because of very low inflation and interest rates. China's emergence gave a strong supply shock to the world economy, which helped create the conditions for excessive debt. Securitization became a deadly weapon in assisting banks to leverage their balance sheets, but it did not cause the crisis. I argue that if the changes brought to the global economy by China's emergence had been better appreciated at the time they were happening, then, armed with this understanding, Western financial policymakers would probably have seen things differently. Better policy decisions might have been taken, with results that could have avoided the crisis altogether, or at least greatly modified its effects. In particular, if Western central banks and politicians had better appreciated the size and strength of the supply shock given by China to the global economic system, they would not have taken fright at the stable prices which occurred in the early part of the millennium. Instead of accommodating these stable prices by reducing interest rates and adding liquidity to an economic system already overloaded with it, they might have felt able to adopt a wiser policy of keeping savings rates at higher and more attractive levels, thereby encouraging investor prudence, reducing upward pressure on asset prices, and forestalling the "search for yield" which became such a strong feature of the run-up to the financial crash of 2008. The financial crisis was not inevitable. It was man-made. But people in high places allowed it to happen, because they were slow to appreciate the nature and extent of the fundamental changes brought by China to the way the world economy works.

Another part of the story of China and the credit crisis concerns the effect of the crisis on China's economy. The crisis brought a collapse in demand in the two principal markets for China's exports—the United States and Europe. In turn, this forced China's leaders to realize that the Chinese economy must be rebalanced, and China's potentially huge domestic demand must be released. The size, unsophistication, and immaturity of China's economy mean that a major change in the shape of the economy could take longer, perhaps much longer, than China's trade partners would like. Although the economic stimulus unleashed in China in November 2008 does assure the relatively rapid recovery of the Chinese economy from the global economic slowdown, the rebalancing of the global economy is not going to be easy to achieve and may produce unanticipated and dangerous side effects. How this economic rebalancing occurs, and how long it takes, is a key factor determining the success of China's continued growth and development after the credit crisis, and also has a vitally important bearing on the prospects for global growth in the next five to 10 years. As James Kynge comments in his Foreword, there are already encouraging signs of robust household and business demand within China which does not depend on exports. The strength and composition of Chinese import growth over the next year or two is one vital indicator of the emergence of strong, autonomous Chinese private demand.

As well as forcing key changes in China's economy, the crisis is affecting its regional profile in Asia and its world posture. China has suddenly appeared in the limelight, from behind the shadow of the United States, as a major force in world affairs. I turn from the impact of the crisis on China's economy to examining the changes brought by the crisis in some of the most important global institutions, in which a newly assertive China is becoming highly active. The Chinese are making their presence felt in the debate over important global institutions, the role of the dollar, and other central matters. Before the crisis, these were matters reserved for discussion and decision among the United States superpower and its G8 allies—chiefly Germany and Japan. The emergence of China as a global player will profoundly affect the configuration of power and influence in the world, and the role of developing countries. I analyze China's impact on the major multilateral institutions, discuss the much-debated role of the dollar as the world currency, and examine China's changing position with respect to three key geographical constituencies—the United States, Asia, and the emerging world.

Chinese Leadership

Until the crisis, China tried to avoid suggestions that its size and fast growth were bringing the role and responsibilities of global leadership. But the crisis has forced China to recognize that it cannot avoid a leadership role any longer. Can China rise to the challenge of global leadership? Can a police state ruled by a communist dictatorship command the admiration of nations still under the influence of the American, French, and English Revolutions? China may be prepared to learn from its major global partners to improve mutual understanding and communication. But another critical success factor for China's continued development is the evolution of China's governing system towards generally accepted norms of justice, equity, and the rule of law, away from the arbitrary, unaccountable exercise of power. Yet, although multi-party democracy is one road to a modern civilized society, it may not be the only one. The West should not assume that China is doomed simply because its system is different.

I argue that the crisis has changed China's view of the West, undermining the perception of Western superiority which had gained ground in China since the 1990s, and replacing it with China's own history and philosophy as an inspiration for China's search for meaning and identity. Moreover, the lessons and ideas of China's past as an influence for the future will be shared more widely. China's size, the significance of Chinese civilization, and the competence of its people have always seemed to indicate that the increase of Chinese influence on the West would be not a question of if, but of when and how. The effect of the crisis and China's much-increased global influence will be to turn the recent one-way traffic of Western ideas to China into a two-way exchange and sharing of economic and philosophical approaches.

China Goes Global

A few months after the Belgrade consulate bombing, in November 1999, China announced it had reached agreement with the United States over the terms of China's accession to the World Trade Organization (WTO). Although it took a couple more years to dot all the i's and cross all the t's, that moment, in November 1999, was when China crossed the Rubicon to join the rest of the world. Suddenly China promised to become an easier, less risky place for foreign companies to do business in.

Through the 1990s, many large multinationals—such as Kingfisher, Metro, Rewe, Tesco, and Carrefour from Europe, and Walmart from America—had opened offices in Hong Kong to buy from Chinese factories. From late 1999, China inside the WTO looked set to become the West's Aladdin's cave, providing first a stream, then a torrent of everyday products to Western consumers at prices which fattened multi-national margins and drove down shop-floor prices. The story of Aladdin and his magic lamp was borrowed in mid-1999 by Jack Ma for his China export company Alibaba based in Hangzhou, near Shanghai. Alibaba started using the Internet to facilitate the sourcing by Western importers of Chinese factory products, aiming its services at Western importers who were too small to establish their own buying operations in China, and at Chinese factories based all over China who lacked direct access to Western buyers. Jack Ma caught the start of a huge wave of Chinese products that hit Western markets in the early years of the millennium. In 2007 Alibaba listed on the Hong Kong stock market; in 2008 it reported net profits of RMB 1.2 billion (US$177 million), and in April 2009 it was valued at nearly US$5 billion.[9] Alibaba's startling success mirrors China's own meteoric trade growth from the late 1990s, when it agreed to terms with American negotiators for joining the WTO. That moment shifted China's impact on the rest of the world into high gear, and that was when the world economic system started to change.

Jack Ma and Alibaba anticipated what would happen, but people in the West, who lacked a knowledge of China's size and dynamism, did not foresee the size of the shock given to the Western economic system by China. For most, the consciousness of China's economic significance has only grown gradually over the last 10 years. It is the credit crisis that has made most of us realize that the balance of global economic power really has started to shift from the developed, Western world, led by the US, towards the newly industrializing countries, led by China. But our memories are short. We forget how very different the world was only a decade ago, and we may overlook the extent to which rapid changes in world economic power can also quickly change who influences world affairs.

Economic Upheaval

China's accession to the WTO started a huge upheaval in the world economy. We will see how this economic upheaval occurred, and why it played an important role in the self-administered financial collapse of the United States. It took a series of policy mistakes, mainly in the United States, to unleash the greed and irresponsibility which precipitated the financial disaster. These policy mistakes were based on a misinterpretation of economic and market signals by key decision-makers, of which the errors of judgment made by the Federal Reserve Bank in Washington, the most powerful decision-maker of all, were the most destructive. But if the changes wrought in Western economies by globalization, in particular by China's supply shock, had been understood at the time, then it would have been possible to set policies in place which averted disaster and preserved the large gains of globalization without having to suffer the huge downside. The financial crash, and the pain and suffering it has caused, could probably have been avoided. The post-crash writings of former Federal Reserve Chairman Alan Greenspan, aimed at finding reasons for the financial crash (reasons preferably unconnected to his own 18-year tenure as head of the US central bank), indicate the low level of significance he continues to attach to these international developments, which actually provided the economic foundation for the crisis. Like a huge dinosaur at the top of the food chain, the years of US global dominance and economic success had dulled its sensitivity to being ambushed by events. Its capacity for sensing hostile developments larger than itself, over which it had no control, atrophied for want of use, so that when a monster threat came along, it grossly underestimated its size and miscalculated its own ability to avert or manage it.

The speed of the financial and economic collapse of the advanced Western nations created an economic and political power vacuum affecting all of the world's key institutions and mechanisms, into which new power from emerging countries, led by China, has begun to flow. For years, countries such as China, India, and Brazil, rich in history and culture, with huge resources and populations, argued for a bigger say in how the world is run. But they lacked the financial clout to persuade the developed countries, led by the United States, to listen to their requests for a fairer representation in global decision-making institutions, such as the International Monetary Fund (IMF) and the G8. Now, thanks to the credit crisis, China's sudden emergence as a great

Figure 1.1   Major Foreign Holders of US Dollar Debt (April 2009)

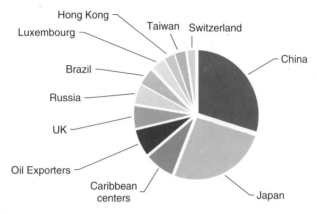

Source: US Treasury

financial power has changed that. Within a few short years, China has become easily the largest external creditor of a United States with huge future financing requirements (see Figure 1.1). Anyone who has been a middle-class teenager knows that if you want money and you don't have any, then you have to do a deal with your parents. If your parents are sensible and far-sighted, they won't make you, the child, feel resentful for taking their money. If they're not so smart, the relationship between parent and child can sour rapidly and permanently. China has to be careful how it treats the United States which needs lots of cash. But the United States, previously in denial about overspending and real estate prices, is now in denial about the extent of its reliance on the foreign funding that must inevitably follow from its overspending, a large part of which must come from outsiders—Russia, Brazil, the Gulf states, Japan, and in particular China, who since 2006 has been the largest buyer of US debt apart from the US Government itself. A US Treasury spokesman recently estimated that the United States Government was looking for China to buy 30 percent of America's multitrillion-dollar debt issues over the next few years. In 2008, one of America's most perceptive and experienced journalists, James Fallows, interviewed the US-educated chief executive of China's sovereign wealth fund China Investment Corporation, Gao Xiqing. "Be nice to the countries that lend you money," was what Mr. Gao said during the interview, and this became the title of the interview that was published in December 2008 in the American current affairs journal *Atlantic Monthly*.[10]

Some Americans have responded to Mr. Gao's request, that they be nice to him and his Chinese banker colleagues, by arguing that China has nowhere to invest with its dollars except in the United States, and the United States is doing China a favor by absorbing China's huge investing needs. This argument misses an important point. Beyond the immediate short term, China can find sensible alternatives to investing new money in the United States. One such alternative is for China to stop generating such large foreign exchange surpluses, as its currency and its imports gradually rise, thereby reducing the quantity of freely investable reserves. Another alternative is to start allocating more of its reserves to domestic projects, as many of the Chinese Government's domestic critics have urged it to do. One such project, which requires very large financial commitments, but would have a very high rate of return to the Chinese economy and Chinese society, would be the funding of a comprehensive Chinese social security system. This large-scale project requires an upfront Chinese currency investment in domestic Chinese securities of several hundred billion in US dollar equivalent terms—enough to put a big dent in China's ability to buy American debt. In fact, a Chinese think-tank closely associated with the government published in January 2009 its estimate of the scope and funding of projects aimed at providing China with a modern system of social security benefits. Their estimate of the budget at the time of writing was 5.74 trillion yuan, or US$840 billion at current exchange rates by 2020.[11] Other large projects relate to China's defense spending, including the recently announced decision to build a blue-water navy which includes aircraft carriers.

The realistic future is that China might not stop investing in the United States altogether, but Chinese funds available for US dollar investment will likely diminish, as China, feeling it is already over-invested in American assets, reweights its geographical investment allocations and finds many productive uses at home and elsewhere for its wealth. The following report, which appeared on Bloomberg Television on June 13, 2009, may be a sign of things to come:

Russia has full confidence in the dollar and there are no immediate plans to switch to a new reserve currency, Finance Minister Alexei Kudrin said. "It's too early to speak of an alternative" to the dollar, Kudrin said in Lecce, Italy, in a television interview today after meeting with finance chiefs from the Group of Eight nations. The fundamentals of the dollar are still in "good shape."

Russia's central bank said on June 10 some reserves may be moved from US Treasuries into International Monetary Fund debt, reiterating comments made last month by Kudrin. That drove Treasuries and the dollar lower. Kudrin said yesterday that Russia's announcement on May 26 to buy US$10 billion of IMF bonds did not represent "a significant change" in his country's stance on the dollar. The dollar declined against a majority of the most-traded currencies as Brazil and Russia joined China in saying they would shift some US$70 billion of reserves from US Treasuries into multicurrency bonds.[12]

If some foreign investors cash in their dollar investments, more of American funding needs over the next five years—which will amount to several trillion US dollars, on top of the roughly US$11 trillion of debt already outstanding—will have to be found from its own insurance companies and mutual funds. Funding America's debt may require returns on American assets to rise significantly, as much to maintain the everyday confidence of world markets in the international value of the dollar as to attract the necessary additional funding from other major surplus countries, led by Japan, the Gulf states, and China. Given growing investor fears that the only way out for America will be currency debasement and inflation, these higher returns would have to be after inflation, or real returns. If American real interest rates rise significantly, the cost of servicing, say, US$15 trillion of American debt could increase within five years to as much as 10 percent of American GDP, taking up one-quarter of the combined Federal and State spending budget and making an even bigger financial hole for America to climb out of.

The point made by the CEO of the China Investment Corporation is that Americans have to become realistic, and face up to where they are. China's recent proposal of a new world currency to replace the dollar is an expression of China's refusal to go on buying dollars to finance excessive American spending. The United States can't conduct its relationship with China from a position of dominance any longer. Neither can it choose to walk away. It has to stay committed and listen to what China, and other emerging countries, are saying. Because China holds the whip hand over American financing, and is shaping up to be the leader of both the developing world and Asia, Chinese influence over all aspects of world affairs will go on increasing. China is already showing the strength and self-confidence to use its position to set new agendas and rally a broad international consensus behind them. That is one reason why this book's title is *China and the Credit Crisis*.

The last time America thought that its dominance might be challenged was by Japan in the early 1980s, when the Japanese economy was booming and America was just starting to recover from the deep recession caused by the second oil shock of 1979. But Japan's stock market and economy collapsed, and the Japanese economy turned out to be a house of cards. Is the same true of China's?

I examine the impact of the financial crisis and the global downturn on the Chinese economy, and conclude that, as a result of the difficult, painful, and fundamental reforms carried out (starting a decade ago in the Chinese banking sector), of the huge size of China's pool of savings, and of the limited exchangeability of the Chinese currency and the restrictions on flows of capital into and out of China, the Chinese economy can withstand the external economic shock caused by a collapse in demand for its exports. In fact, thanks to the massive economic stimulus organized by the Chinese Government late in 2008, financed from China's huge savings, China will be the first large economy in the world to emerge from the economic slowdown of 2008. But I argue that China's high savings rate will be slow to change, due in part to China's demographics, as well as to the inertia of custom. A widely anticipated and desired big shift towards private spending as a driver of China's growth may not happen as quickly as developed countries hope.

In 1944 the 44 countries allied in the World War against Germany and Japan, led by the United States, Britain, and the Soviet Union, met at Bretton Woods in scenic New Hampshire, America, to work out a new governance architecture which could support the massive task of reconstruction and development that faced the world at the end of the war. The participants in the Bretton Woods conference established several multilateral bodies to govern affairs between countries. Possibly the most important of these bodies was the IMF, set up as the central global body to oversee and maintain the world's financial architecture. From the beginning, the United States had by far the largest stake in the IMF which, with an 85 percent voting majority required to pass a new resolution, and with support from its close allies Britain, Canada, and other European countries, became a blocking stake which today stands at just under 17 percent.

As the fall of the Soviet Union and the US's own economic success propelled the latter into a position of even greater dominance, it became increasingly intolerant of the limits placed upon its discretionary power by the multilateral organizations founded in the surge of altruism and hope which marked the end of the war. These organizations gradually started to fall into neglect, with resolutions ignored and funding unmet. But as the United States now weakens, a place is being found once again for the multilateral organizations as organs of global government and guardians of the developing world. Chapter 4 examines the wind of change which the crisis is blowing through the United Nations (UN), the IMF, and the World Bank. There could be no better sign of the shock effect of the financial crisis on world affairs than the IMF Reform Committee's report of March 2009, which concluded that thorough reorganization of the IMF was called for. It was only in April 2008 that this organization, noted for its staid caution and conservatism, had agreed, after years of foot-dragging, to a minor change in voting rights which modestly favored China, Korea, Mexico, and Turkey at the expense of the United States, Britain, and Germany. But when financial disaster struck Wall Street in September 2008, a Reform Committee was immediately established to examine how the IMF should be reorganized. The Reform Committee's report noted that:

. . . the world needs a multilateral institution at the centre of the world economy to help anchor global financial stability. The International Monetary Fund needs to increase its legitimacy and effectiveness in addressing today's global challenges. Few of the requirements outlined are being met.[13]

The crisis may be revitalizing global governance. The IMF may become a forum where the developed and developing worlds can meet to debate the shape of the world's new economic landscape. Six of the nine members of the 2009 IMF Committee which recommended a big change and enhancement of its role were from the developing world: the finance ministers of South Africa, Indonesia, Mexico, and China; a former IMF deputy director who is an ethnic Egyptian; and an Indian Nobel Prize winner in economics. The Committee's report may eventually fundamentally restructure the IMF, dismissing much of the legacy influence exercised by Europe and the US, and bring it back to its central role, as conceived by the original 1945 blueprint, as a keystone in the global financial architecture. In this role, the IMF could be a powerful guardian of the interests of the developing world led by China and India.

For years, critics of using one country's currency as the dominant means of exchange and as the store of value in an international monetary system have pointed to the inherent impossibility of meeting domestic economic and financial currency needs at the same time as the international requirements for a world currency. Since 1971 a world monetary system based on nothing but the good faith and self-interest of the United States has worked, but at the cost of large disruptions in the global economy. The sudden collapse in demand resulting from America's financial crisis in 2008 has now given rise to huge injections of government credit which have been backed by enormous issues of US dollars to stimulate growth. As the largest foreign holder of American debt, China has expressed its concern that these large money issues could put the dollar firmly on the road to losing its status as a store of value for Chinese savings. Chapter 5 discusses China's proposal to replace the US dollar as the global savings and transacting currency, by replacing it with a global super-currency. Although predictably the proposal has not received much American interest (apart notably from Nobel Prize winning economist Joseph Stiglitz), other countries, including Brazil and Russia, have come out in strong support of such a notion. Does the idea have merit and could Chinese support make it happen? As the United States is not currently in a position to kick difficult ideas into the long grass, the idea of a new global currency probably won't go away. Could this be another area where Americans will be forced to make important compromises?

China and International Relations

The next part of the book examines the effect of the crisis on China's relationships with three key global constituencies: the United States, Asia, and the rest of the emerging world. Hillary Clinton's China visit in February 2009 has already highlighted the seriousness with which the Obama Administration views China. The US is going to go on bumping into China everywhere, and Americans recognize that. For their part, the Chinese have long been ready to view the US as their natural global partner. Now Americans themselves are coming to terms with the realization that they have to do business with China as equals on the global stage. The US may attempt to make a virtue out of a necessity by developing the China relationship as an exclusive, G2-style team which can decide the important global issues on its own. The Chinese, however, will see their relationship with the US not so much as a world government, but rather as a relationship with their most important global partner which has vital global implications.

   The importance for China's international relations of the link with the US certainly extends to China's position in Asia, which is the subject of Chapter 7. The competition for Asian dominance between India, Japan, and China is heating up. India feels it owes nothing to China in terms of size and antiquity of culture; its economy is beginning to grow as fast, and it has the great advantage over China of being the world's largest English-speaking democracy, ruled by law. Japan, still easily the richest Asian country, and still, the world's second largest economy, has been the US's anchor partner in the Pacific since the end of the Second World War. The Japanese feel they don't have to pretend to be the dominant Pacific power, because they are. By offering in March 2009 to lend US$100 billion to the IMF as a necessary quick boost to the IMF's financial firepower, Japan was quick to show its economic power to China. Both India and Japan look down on undemocratic, sprawling China for deeply felt cultural reasons. Both resent and fear China's grasping efforts to control East Asia. Keeping its relations on track with its two Asian rivals may constitute China's toughest foreign policy challenge. Tensions between India, China, and Japan will likely rise. 'It is here that the greatest threats to world peace may lie in the next 50 years. China's relationship with the United States will prove of great significance in keeping a balance between the three great Asian powers.

Meanwhile, by undermining the apparent financial solidity of Western countries and by default reinforcing the financial attractions of China, the credit crisis has given wings to the great project of Chinese unification. Hong Kong and Taiwan, China's most important trade and investment partners, have both played a vital role in China's development. Predictions of disaster in Hong Kong following the end of British rule in 1997 have not been borne out by events. Hong Kong has demonstrably prospered under Chinese rule—a fact which China hopes will not be lost on the Taiwanese. In Taiwan, the victory of the mainland-backed Kuomintang party in the Taiwanese elections in 2008 brought an end to threats of Taiwanese independence. Now that Shanghai and other cities on the mainland can provide a standard of living comparable to, or better than, Taipei, it is probably only a question of time before Taiwan formally joins the mainland. In March 2009, the Chinese Government announced that the world's longest sea-bridge would be built, to link the former colonies Macao and Hong Kong with the Chinese mainland, at an estimated cost of RMB 72.6 billion (around US$10.7 billion at exchange rates at the time of writing). This project is another massive step towards the goal of full unification. Its intended message to recalcitrant Taiwanese opponents to unification with China is, "Why bother—we're too powerful, it's going to happen anyway, and look what the benefits are." Who can deny that?

China's Internal Problems

Although China will soon be the world's second largest economy (see Figure 1.2), it contains more poor people than any country except India. This means that, while it can stand toe-to-toe with America as a large, financially strong, open economy, it is also one of the world's largest developing countries. China has an even closer relationship with the poor, developing world than it does with the rich, developed one. In 2008, China's government went to great lengths and expense in the Beijing Olympic Games to project both to its own people and worldwide an image of a powerful country with an ancient culture, which is returning to its natural position of global leadership. Yet, if you divide China's wealth by its population, the picture of economic

Figure 1.2   Largest Countries by Size of GDP in 2010, 2014 (est.)

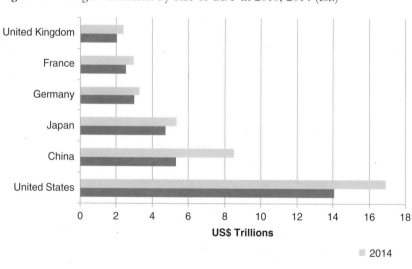

Source: IMF

strength changes quite dramatically. On a wealth-per-head basis, the World Bank in 2008 ranked China as a low middle-income country, along with 54 others, including Albania, Bhutan, Egypt, the Congo, Tunisia, and India.[14] By 2050 China's economy may be nearly twice as large as the US economy. But when adjusted for population, China in 2050 will still rank behind Mexico, Italy, and Brazil, and only just ahead of Turkey, Vietnam, and Iran. China is a huge and powerful country, but its enormous population is mostly very poor.

The sharp contrast between increasing global power and influence on the one hand and domestic vulnerability on the other gives China two distinctly different personalities. One personality is the country with the world's largest foreign reserves which is starting to have a say in everything, and with whom Hillary Clinton wants to be a global partner. The other personality is that of the leader of the third world which contains more poor people than the combined populations of Western Europe and the United States, including between 100 and 200 million who live below the official bread line. Figure 1.3, below, which ranks the G8 countries by national income per head of population, shows China lagging well behind Russia and the other G8 countries, in contrast to Figure 1.2 above, which shows China as the world's second largest economy in absolute terms. This dual personality has large implications for how the country will use its power to develop

Figure 1.3   G8 plus China—US$ per Capita 2008

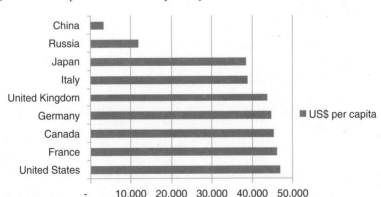

Source: IMF

its global position. China sees itself as being in a unique position both to partner with the rich world on the one hand, and continue Mao's mission of leading the poor world on the other. China's need for natural resources and its desire to complete Taiwan's international isolation, rather than charity and a sense of world citizenship, have been the main considerations driving China's relationships with poor countries. China's drive into Africa since 2003 has been fast, ruthless, and highly effective in securing strategic access to the huge range and quantities of natural resources on which China relies for future development. Chapter 8 examines China's partnership with the other poor populous countries in Asia, Latin America, and Africa, and its leadership of the developing world.

China's Growing Leadership Position

The final chapters of the book examine China's capacity and appetite for the role of global leadership which the crisis has forced on it, and the effect that the crisis has had on Chinese ideas, both about the West as a model for development, and about themselves. The Chinese have regarded the financial crisis as a Western phenomenon, which has hardly scratched their own financial system. Although they were dismayed in 2008 at the real economic damage done to their export industries by the collapse in demand in their main overseas markets, the United States and Europe, they saw an opportunity to advance their global status and economic capacity. But the failure in early June 2009 by one of China's most important natural resource companies Chinalco to complete a US$19.5 billion transaction with huge Western mining company Rio Tinto, which would have given the Chinese a significant stake in Rio Tinto as well as rights in some of Rio's most valuable mines, shows that China's global progress won't all be plain sailing. Can the Chinese persuade the West that their ascendancy is to be welcomed more than it is to be feared and resisted? Can they turn their economic muscle into sustainable leadership?

    As the interaction of this huge and ancient country with the rest of the world spreads and deepens, a question arises as to what effect China's unique culture and values will have on other countries, particularly on those outside Asia. Will non-Asian countries come to regard China as more than a very large country with a big pile of money? Will Chinese values of harmony follow Chinese medicine overseas to bring Chinese culture to the benefit of mankind? Or will China be more changed by the world, than the world changed by China? The Jewish people, wherever they end up in the world, have been noted for keeping their blood pure and their customs intact by intermarriage. But it is said that China, who received Jewish influxes very early on into the north-west part of China where the Chinese trade routes with Central Asia and Europe originated, is the only country (with the possible exception of the United States) where the Jews have been completely absorbed culturally by their host country. Chinese civilization developed independently from Europe, and China probably sent many more messages along the ancient trade route to the West, the Silk Route, than it received. The remarkable work of the British biologist turned Sinophile Dr. Joseph Needham at Cambridge University in England, which was spread over half a century between 1940 and his death in the early 1990s, surprised Chinese as much as Westerners by demonstrating that Chinese technology dating from centuries before Christ was far in advance of anything known in the West, and probably inspired many Western technological developments previously thought to be of indigenous origin.[15] China developed a culture thousands of years ago which matched or exceeded that of the Romans in material terms, and challenged that of the Greeks in philosophical terms. The period of foreign incursion into China, from the 1830s until 1945, did not last long enough or go deep enough to destroy China's independent culture. Mao's Cultural Revolution went further in destroying the old Chinese ways of life, but only lasted for 12 years—not enough either to permanently eradicate millennia of Chinese civilization. Chinese attitudes to the West have changed since the crisis. Even though many of today's Chinese may be ignorant of their country's history, the ideas and attitudes of the Chinese today owe everything to their long history. Isolated by its language as much as its long habit of looking inward, China today remains starkly different from other non-Asian countries, creating plenty of opportunities—as global economic and social cooperation becomes ever closer—for misunderstanding and disagreement as well as mutual enlightenment and enrichment.

A person who had said in 1979 or even in 1989 that China would be the world's third largest economy in 2009 and a superpower to rank with the United States in terms of global influence, and that this huge change would be accomplished peacefully, would have invited frank disbelief. Yet the impossible has happened and is happening.

China's emergence created a precondition for the credit crisis. In turn, the credit crisis has acted as a tipping point for the shift from West to East. It will be no easier to predict the next 30 years than it was in 1980 to see what the world would look like in 2010. This book's premise is that this shouldn't stop us trying.

Endnotes

1. "NATO Bombed Chinese Deliberately," John Sweeney, Jens Holsoe, and Ed Vulliamy, *The Observer*, October 17, 1999.
2. Executive Memorandum #600, the Heritage Foundation, May 28, 1999.
3. "Downed Spy Plane Takes Sino–US Relations to New Level," Nick Papadopoulos, *Time*, April 2, 2001.
4. Editorial, *The Times*, February 23, 2009.
5. "Compliments, not Controversy, Mark Hillary Clinton's Beijing Visit," Jane Macartney, *The Times*, February 23, 2009.
6. Statement on Bilateral Meeting with President Hu of China, White House, Office of the Press Secretary, April 1, 2009.
7. *People's Daily*, April 2, 2009.
8. CNBC, March 2009.
9. Alibaba annual report 2008, Hong Kong Stock Exchange, April 2009.
10. "Be Nice to the Countries that Lend You Money," James Fallows, *Atlantic Monthly*, December 2008.
11. *People's Daily*, January 20, 2009.
12. Bloomberg Television, June 12, 2009.
13. Committee on IMF Governance Reform, Final Report, March 24, 2009.
14. IBRD Data and Statistics.
15. *The Man Who Loved China*, Simon Winchester, Harper Collins, 2008.

CHAPTER

2

Did China Cause the Credit Crisis?

C hina did not cause the credit crisis. But without China, the credit crisis could not have happened. Too much debt was what caused the credit crisis. But people should appreciate that China's emergence, and the supply-side shock that it brought, played a vital role in creating the low interest rates which encouraged huge over-borrowing. Nearly one in every five people on this planet is Chinese. So China's formal emergence into the world economy in the late 1990s was bound to be the biggest part of globalization, the process by which the people of the world are being gradually unified into a single society and beginning to function together. In fact, China's emergence was an event big enough to change the way the world economy worked. The effect was hugely beneficial, but came with the risk of upsetting the world economy. Unfortunately neither the effect, nor the risk, were really understood at the time they were happening, at least in the Western nations where the financial crisis occurred. A combination of wrong policies and systemic failures, analyzed in this chapter, meant that the potential downside to China's emergence materialized, and some of the beneficial effects were washed out to sea.

China Joins the World Trade Organization

Following years of negotiation, in 1999 China finally decided to sign up to the world economy by joining the organization that sets the rules by which countries trade with each other—the World Trade Organization—thereby for the first time, and irretrievably, tying China's vast economy to the rest of the world. I use the word "irretrievably" because, although in theory China could cancel its WTO membership, in practice such a step would be economically highly disadvantageous to China, and would also be inconsistent with China's own dignity and sense of honor. China's WTO accession marked a victory for Chinese reformers over the Beijing bureaucrats, who had for years successfully avoided WTO membership by appealing to China's tradition of splendid isolation in order to protect their own monopolies and vested interests, together with those of their many corporate and political allies. The notion that China could be dependent on other countries, rather than the rest of the world depending on and looking up to China, ran (and still runs) counter to long-entrenched Chinese habits and beliefs. Appeals to this notion helped Chinese conservatives and the monopolists to delay China's entry to the WTO.

Fifty years earlier, Mao had used this Chinese spirit of independence to rebuild China's pride and self-belief, although his search for self-reliance brought an economic autarky which nearly destroyed China. It took another very forceful leader, Prime Minister Zhu Rongji, backed by Chinese President Jiang Zemin, to push the WTO through. So strong was the opposition inside China to bringing the Chinese economy within global multilateral rules that onlookers doubted a successful outcome to China's final negotiations with the United States until the very last moment. But pushed through it was, and the announcement in November 1999 of China's WTO accession not only opened up China's market, but placed China's huge labor force fully at the disposal of the world economy.

Although both the practical effects of the negotiations and the spirit of openness that lay behind them were widely applauded, the full effect of China's WTO accession was unfortunately not well anticipated or understood at the time it happened. In fact, the economic effects were big enough to give a major shock to the world economy, significantly shifting the global economic balance towards higher growth and lower inflation. For a time, the effect of China's accession to the world economy was to add both stability and prosperity. The combination of falling inflation, together with high, apparently sustainable growth surprised and confused economists. They coined a term to describe the effect: "The Great Moderation."[1] But California-based fund managers PIMCO used another, more perceptive expression for the global economic system that emerged early in the decade which started in 2000. They called it "stable disequilibrium."[2] China's accession to the global system brought risks as well as rewards. Because the true nature of these risks was not appreciated, inappropriate policies were adopted, which created an unchecked appetite for risk that unhinged and broke the US financial system, in turn generating a global recession.

The first Chinese shock was caused by the manufacture of everyday goods in China at a fraction of Western cost, and the export of these goods in enormous quantities to the main consumer markets in the West. Consumer goods of all kinds were made and packaged in China, and imported from China into Western supermarkets and chain stores where they were sold at extremely competitive prices. By 2000, the volumes of Chinese products entering Western economies were already large enough to materially affect Western price levels (see Figure 2.1).[3] Lower Chinese prices also affected other goods that competed with or substituted for Chinese imports, as well as products that used these cheaper goods as inputs into other products. The downward pressure on Western price levels from Chinese manufacture was powerful, multiplying itself throughout Western economies, bringing households greater affordability and higher standards of living, and increasing profits to importers and Western retailers.[4] From the late 1990s, China's economy also impacted Western labor markets, as Western factory owners were forced to meet Chinese competition either by leaving that industry or by closing production in the West and moving it to

Figure 2.1   US Consumer Price Index 1990–2007—Average of US City Prices

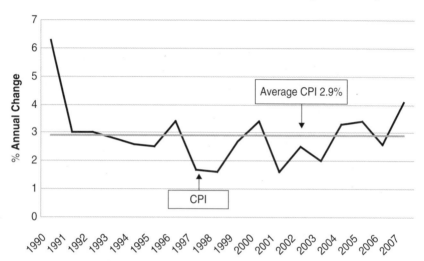

Source: US Bureau of Labor Statistics

China—in either case forcing Western workers to choose between changing their jobs and becoming unemployed.

These effects rippled and multiplied through Western economies, reducing prices for a wide range of everyday products, raising unemployment and putting pressure on wages for factory workers. Unskilled workers in the United States and most of Europe saw little addition to their salaries between 2000 and 2007, even as their economies boomed. In the 10 years between 1995 and 2005, average wages in the United States, when adjusted for price changes, rose at an annual rate of 0.5 percent.[5] But lower prices for many everyday goods, together with much easier and more available credit, compensated Western workers for the weakening of their pricing power in the labor marketplace. In many cases workers' living standards rose, although their wages were virtually static in real terms.

Analyses of the financial crisis to date have underestimated the role played by China's global emergence in creating the economic background to the financial crisis of 2008. China's sheer size and the efficiency and competitiveness of its export industry meant that its global impact changed the world economy. Western economists and policymakers, who had no knowledge or experience of China, were caught by surprise, and continued to underestimate China's economic impact, even after it had become abundantly clear to any factory owner in Mexico, the US, or Europe who had had to close down or move production to the East, and even after Treasury Secretary John Snow had started fulminating over China's trade practices in 2003.[6] Among those who were in a position to change policies in the West, how many had been to see China's export factories? A short stay in a five-star hotel in Beijing or Shanghai could not convey the vast, intense reality of China or the magnitude of its impact.

Bad Policy

The China price effect showed up in the statistics that economists and government officials used to monitor prices. This price effect was important in persuading Western monetary authorities, particularly in the US, that price inflation had disappeared and that monetary stimulus, including lower interest rates, was necessary to stimulate growth and absorb unemployment. From 2002 it was believed necessary to use monetary stimulus to offset the possibility of falling prices, which are dreaded by policymakers because they can persuade consumers to delay buying, thereby making a trap from which escaping can become increasingly difficult. In fact, at this time Western economies were not entering a deflationary demand trap but were being subjected to a big one-off external shock from globalization, in particular from China's supply shock. The re-emergence of price inflation around 2005 showed that the reports of its death had been greatly exaggerated. The monetary stimulus was unnecessary and helped to create the disastrous real estate bubble at the heart of the crisis, by making buying a house appear a much more attractive form of saving than a bank deposit which carried virtually no return.

In retrospect, the correct economic policy to be followed, as the world recovered from the 2001 economic slowdown, would have been to maintain a monetary policy that rewarded savers and deterred excessive borrowing. The actual policy followed, of accommodating downward pressure on prices with a much looser monetary policy, including lower interest rates, was wrong. Former American Deputy Treasury Secretary and leading investment banker Roger Altman expresses this point clearly in an article he wrote in the leading American journal *Foreign Affairs* in February 2009: "Conventional wisdom attributes the crisis to the collapse of housing prices and the subprime mortgage markets in the United States. This is not correct; these were themselves the consequence of another problem. The crisis' underlying cause was the (invariably lethal) combination of very low interest rates and unprecedented levels of liquidity."[7]

Altman attributes the liquidity problem to the enormous financial surpluses run by some Asian economies and oil producers, but he does not associate the disastrously low interest rate regime of Alan Greenspan with the deflationary symptoms which China's earlier supply shock caused. If the nature of the shock had been understood for what it was at the time, then policymakers would not have worried so much about the possibility of deflation, or falling prices.

As it was, policymakers began to believe that their wise policies had produced a new economic utopia. The British Chancellor at that time, Gordon Brown proclaimed "the end of boom and bust." His speech to the British Labour Party conference in October 2000 is worth quoting:

No return to short-termism. No return to Tory boom and bust . . . So it is not by accident, but by our actions, that we now have the lowest inflation for over 30 years and around the lowest long term interest rates for 35 years, and a mortgage bill on average £1,000 lower than under Tory interest rates . . .[8]

Since 2008 and the financial and economic collapse in Britain, Brown has been much criticized for his repeated use in the early millennium years of the political slogan "an end to boom and bust." But he was not alone in thinking that his policies had permanently changed his country's economy for the better. Fed Chairman Greenspan's disastrous economic policy between 2002 and 2004, of keeping interest rates much too low for much too long, and his refusal to contemplate pricking the huge bubble in house prices which resulted, arose from the same erroneous belief.

The second shock from China, which followed the first by several years, was to capital markets, particularly the US debt markets. As Chinese profits from trade grew, US dollars and euros started piling up in China. These swelling hard currency reserves needed a home, which was found by re-lending the surpluses back to the developed world, particularly the Americans. China became the largest buyer of US debt (not counting the US Government's own repurchases after the crisis to reduce interest rates). As interest rates are determined in part by the supply of and demand for capital, a stream of additional supply from Chinese capital surpluses placed continual downward pressure on US and European bond yields. Low interest rates push up asset prices, including the prices of real estate. The additional supply of capital from oil producers and emerging countries, led by China, drove already low US Treasury yields down further, aggravating the impact on asset prices. From 2003 we find the "search for yield" appearing as a driver of investment behavior in investment commentaries, becoming widely used and recognized in the years following. The "search for yield" drove some investors to start taking reckless, imprudent risks, the downside of China's global impact. But although China played a vital role in creating the circumstances which led to the financial crisis, the crisis occurred because of poor decisions by Western policymakers and reckless behavior by bankers and investors. China's emergence brought great benefits to China, the rest of Asia, other emerging economies who sold to China, and to Western consumers—in fact, to the world economy.

Would Chinese Currency Revaluation Have Helped?

As reserves piled up in the Chinese treasury, could trouble have been avoided if China had allowed its currency to float upwards against the US dollar? This would have had the effect of making Chinese exports more expensive, thereby reducing the benefit to Western consumers of inexpensive Chinese-made goods, but reducing also the impact of China's export industry on Western consumer and capital markets. Could this have averted the credit crisis? An early Chinese currency revaluation may also have limited the huge, inflationary inflows of speculative capital which found their way into China's banks from 2004, betting on an upward shift of China's currency against the dollar. A one-off revaluation of the Chinese yuan of 30 percent in 2003 or 2004 against Western currencies could have disrupted Chinese trade patterns, reducing by some degree the rate of Chinese export growth, mitigating the downward impact of China's export prices on Western price levels, and increasing the attractiveness of imports to Chinese buyers by making them significantly cheaper.

But the effect of Chinese currency appreciation on Chinese trade patterns would have been restricted by China's role as a huge manufacturing entrepot in Asia. About 60 percent of Chinese imports consist of components and semi-finished products (such as specialist computer chips and car bodies), mostly from China's high-technology neighbors Taiwan, Japan, and South Korea, which are assembled into final products in China and re-exported. A stronger Chinese currency, which makes Chinese imports cheaper and Chinese exports more expensive, allows a choice to multinationals that export product components into China and re-export finished goods from China to developed markets, to manage their prices to maintain their final end-market volumes. In fact, China did start to liberalize its currency in July 2005, replacing the hard fix against the US dollar which had been maintained since the late 1990s with a gradual, managed appreciation against a basket of currencies made up of its main foreign trading partners (America, Europe, and Japan). By the time China halted the managed revaluation of its currency—three years later—in an attempt to help Chinese exporters hit by the negative effects of collapsing US demand, the Chinese currency was trading against the dollar about 20 percent higher. World Bank research done in 2006 and 2007 shows that most Chinese exporters were able to manage this significant upward re-pricing of their products against the currency of their then most important export market by finding new efficiencies and raising product quality.[9] In other words,

China's continual improvements in productivity, added to low Chinese labor costs, could deal with a significantly stronger Chinese currency.

The dominating role played by large foreign multinationals in China's export industry, and the extent of their commitment there, plus the ability of Chinese factories to manage a stronger Chinese currency, invites the conclusion that, if the Chinese had agreed to American demands for a large, one-off revaluation of the Chinese currency, then the consequences might have been only to defer the impact on Western economies of China's opening up. Given the combination of contemporary policies, attitudes, and circumstances in the West, particularly in the United States, the ultimately disastrous outcome would probably not have been avoided, although its timing may have been delayed.

Seeds of the Crisis

Attempts by Western bankers and politicians to blame the crisis on excess capital generated by Asian thrift sound like a driver blaming his car accident on the man who bought him a drink. Accountants and insolvency practitioners invariably place the blame for avoidable company failures on the managers of the companies concerned. At the country level, the same rule applies. Better economic understanding, leading to different economic policies, would have cut Gordon Brown's premature triumphalism short, and would have averted the crisis. The great benefits of globalization, especially China's emergence as a major trading nation, could have been preserved, instead of being partially washed out to sea along with the Western financial system. So why weren't they?

Some of the seeds of the crisis were sown much earlier, in the revolution wrought by Ronald Reagan in America and Margaret Thatcher in Britain in the 1980s. After a long period in the US of high inflation and economic weakness, which created a strong preference among American investors over their own currency for gold and Swiss francs, the story of the 1980s was the restoration of America's belief in itself, by way of the defeat of communism and the re-establishment of the United States as a prosperous economy. The result of this decade of a resurgent America was to entrench the idea of free, unregulated markets as an ideology firmly anchored in the public mind.

The 1970s were unkind to the United States. The twin blows of the impeachment of an American President at home, and abroad the ignominious withdrawal from Saigon following complete defeat at the hands of the communist North Vietnamese, traumatized Americans. The doubling of oil prices in 1979 left the developed, oil-dependent world with a sense of helplessness. Against this background, America's unsuccessful attempt at a helicopter rescue of American hostages held by Iran brought national despair to a head. In 1980, as in 2008, Americans, optimists by nature, were ready for anything that was different and promised better. The stage was set for a message of hope, and a new start in a different direction. Enter Californian Governor Ronald Reagan, with a message delivered in the 1980 presidential election by one of the most charismatic and popular American politicians of all time. The message, greeted with almost hysterical fervor, was that the heavy hand of government had failed, and should be replaced by the invisible hand of the market. High taxes should give way to high growth.

But Reagan had another message, of even greater force, which played directly into entrenched American feelings of isolationism and moral superiority: that the forces of good, represented by the American libertarian, democratic tradition, were ranged against the forces of evil, personified by repressive communism. The forces of good must prevail. This call to arms made Reagan into an American hero, making his free-market message all the more seductive. The massive military spending of the United States in the early 1980s brought the Soviets close to bankruptcy and defeated the Soviet system, but placed the American budget under huge strain. Federal Reserve Governor Paul Volcker's tight monetary policies, which were aimed at stamping out inflation, plus the need to import the capital that the US required, raised the US dollar to all-time highs against the other major world currencies. But after years of soul-searching and apparent decline, Americans were delighted by the ultra-strong dollar. Government involvement in the economy was accepted as being bad and un–American. A wave of deregulation hit the economy, from airlines to banking. Taxes came down, radically increasing the economy's growth potential. As Volcker's strong medicine worked, inflation receded. The economy started to grow in leaps and bounds. Worries about huge US deficits receded.

A new economic philosophy established itself, based on individual enterprise and money making, the absence of government, and the magical ability of the market to grow the economy by bringing together through trade the self-interest of the multitude. The advocates of this "hands-off" philosophy called themselves Neoclassicists because they believed that their ideas were simply a return to the classical ideas laid out two hundred years before by Adam Smith, the Scottish writer, Glasgow University professor, and advisor and tutor to a Scottish aristocrat, the Duke of Buccleuch.

In Britain, Margaret Thatcher had arrived in 1979 as Prime Minister, with similar ideas of rolling back the State and allowing individual enterprise to flourish. Thatcher in Britain and Reagan in the United States each immediately recognized in the other the same instincts, and encouraged each other during their periods of power throughout the 1980s to defeat communism and remove government influence on the economy, making the new free-market philosophy even more influential. The success of Reagan's and Thatcher's revolutions established firmly in the popular consciousness the notions that government was bad, regulation was bad, and free enterprise was good. An important consequence of these revolutions was the opening of the formerly closed communist societies to Western investment and production methods. By the mid-1990s, foreign multinationals, advised by their management consultants, were introducing new plants and production methods into China. This transfer of knowledge and technology created the foundation that allowed the Chinese economy to accelerate when it joined the WTO.

By 2000, these simple concepts formed the core of an entrenched free-market ideology. In fact Adam Smith, the man who had inspired the new ideology, had written another book before he wrote *The Wealth of Nations*, called *The Theory of Moral Sentiments*, in which he demonstrated the importance of non-profit values, arguing that "humanity, justice, generosity and public spirit, are the qualities most useful to others." As Professor Amartya Sen of Harvard University has pointed out, Smith appears never in his books to have used the term "capitalism," and believed neither in the sufficiency of the market economy nor in the need to accept the dominance of capital.[10] In his most famous book *The Wealth of Nations* he discussed the important role of broader values for the choice of behavior, as well as the importance of institutions.

But the Reagan–Thatcher economic revolutionaries did not care too much for academic niceties. In their pursuit of the ideals of liberty and prosperity, and as they sought the defeat of the evil empire of communism, they took what they needed from whatever came to hand and whatever seemed useful. By the time of the financial crisis in 2008, the association between economic success and unfettered, free markets had become the norm. If further evidence were needed that this notion dominated the thinking of policymakers, then the testimony on October 23, 2008, of former American central bank chief Alan Greenspan before the House Oversight Committee in Washington DC, and its chairman Congressman Henry Waxman, provided it:

> **Oversight Committee Chairman Henry Waxman:** ... Dr. Greenspan ... I'm going to interrupt you. The question I have for you is, you had an ideology. This is your statement. "I do have an ideology. My judgment is that free competitive markets are by far the unrivaled way to organize economies. We have tried regulation, none meaningfully worked." That was your quote. You had the authority to prevent irresponsible lending practices that led to the subprime mortgage crisis. You were advised to do so by many others. And now our whole economy is paying its price. Do you feel that your ideology pushed you to make decisions that you wish you had not made?

> **Alan Greenspan:** I found a flaw in the model that I perceived as the critical functioning structure that defines how the world works.[11]

An unthinking belief in the free-market ideology also governed the thinking of the regulators, particularly the Securities and Exchange

Commission in New York and the Financial Services Authority in London, who between them set the rules for the two dominant financial centers. These two institutions started to compete with each other over who could interfere least in the activities of the big financial players, whether banks or hedge funds. So it happened that a widely held, unquestioning, almost unthinking acceptance of the free-market ideology led to a complete lack of oversight from the financial market policemen. The excesses which led to the financial crisis could only have happened in an environment which scorned oversight.

Moral Hazard

Another necessary condition for the financial crisis was the widespread belief held by the markets that the American Government would not allow anything big to fail, for fear of causing a general or "systemic" financial collapse. This belief has a name—"moral hazard"; so-called because once a sufficient number of market participants believe that the government will intervene on a regular basis in the market, then their perception of risk changes, and so does their behavior, which can become dangerous and destabilizing. Markets are sometimes compared to an almost infinite number of coin tosses. If, on average, the odds from tossing a coin are a 50 percent gain, 50 percent loss, then coin tossers who win or lose several times in succession believe that at some point their luck will turn—even if each coin toss is theoretically independent of the coin toss that preceded it. The knowledge that the market's outcome is on average a fair game keeps market participants honest. But if the coin toss or market odds are 55 percent gain, 45 percent loss, then participants know that, even if they lose short term, they will always come out with a profit, if they play for long enough. The odds are always in their favor, and they will take risks that they wouldn't take if the odds were evenly balanced. If the odds are the other way round, and participants stand to lose on average more times than they win, then players may only participate for short periods in the market, and the market may eventually close. For markets to function well and to be of service to society, the chances faced by participants of being right or wrong must be felt to be about equal, on average over a reasonable time span. A significant moral hazard problem is like a cancer which grows, being at first unnoticeable, but then becoming increasingly invasive until it throttles the life out of the market.

We must go back to August 1987, when the most important job in world banking changed hands, to find the roots of the moral hazard problem. In that month Alan Greenspan replaced the much respected Paul Volcker as the head of the Federal Reserve Board, America's central bank, with responsibility for guarding the integrity of the country's money, consistent as far as possible with a maximum level of employment. Because the US dollar is used to settle trade worldwide, it is the world currency. In consequence, the US Federal Reserve Bank carries a global as well as a national responsibility. Paul Volcker's two terms as head of America's central bank had seen a complete turnaround in American economic and monetary fortunes. But he left Greenspan a difficult situation when he finished his second term. In 1987 Reagan's massive defense spending, plus America's resurgent economic growth, had started to produce signs of economic overheating, as strong demand outstripped productive capacity, and the price level was rising. The new chairman's immediate response to the situation was to tighten monetary policy. He had just succeeded a particularly popular and respected chairman, and was anxious to show the markets that he was in charge. Within two months the tough policy cracked the markets, with the Dow Jones falling a record 22.6 percent on October 19, 1987, following with a further huge fall the next day. The dollar, which had strengthened as American monetary policy tightened, collapsed, as did equity markets. Investors rushed to the relative safety of government credit, and bond markets soared.

The new Fed chairman must have been taken aback by the virulence of the response to his monetary tightening. No matter that within three months markets were back on an even keel, demonstrating that Black Monday, as it became known, was just a necessary and correct, if violent, adjustment to economic overheating and stock market froth. Black Monday went down in the annals of Wall Street as a historic correction, and Wall Street was quick to signal its displeasure to the new chairman, who had many banking and broking friends from his years as an economic advisor and consultant. The aggressive monetary tightening policy pursued by the Fed received a share of the blame for Black Monday. Some of the criticism was directed at the new chairman.

Alan Greenspan remained Fed Chairman for 18 years, serving three six-year terms under four presidents, two of whom were father and son. But never again in his terms of office did he pursue monetary tightening with anything like the aggression that he showed in his first months in office, even though economic expansion threatened to overheat both the American and global economies more than once.

The Collapse of Long-Term Capital Management and the Dot-Com Boom

The next time markets went haywire was not as a result of Fed policy, but an external event. Following a period of turbulence in Asian markets, in 1998 Russia defaulted on its debt. Market volatility soared, and well-established trading expectations were shattered. Within days it became clear that one of New York's largest unregulated funds had gone completely off the rails. Long-Term Capital Management (LTCM), set up by a former bond trader John Meriwether, pursued a highly leveraged strategy based on trading against previously observed market behavior patterns, a strategy that had proved highly profitable for several years. But the Russian debt crisis in August 2008 severed well-established relationships and correlations between different securities, destroying trading patterns and turning profitable arbitrages into huge losses overnight. By September, LTCM found itself with losses on its trading positions which amounted to close to its total capital. Through August and into September the firm moved closer to insolvency, and the directors of the fund raised the alarm with the Federal Reserve Board. After LTCM had failed to raise new capital, a consortium, led by Warren Buffett and Goldman Sachs, smelling an opportunity, offered to pay the partners $250 million for the fund. This offer was rejected, because the partners suspected they would get a much better deal from the government. They were right. Greenspan decided he could not take the risk posed to the main banking counterparties by the fund's collapse, and organized a rescue of the fund by way of an injection of capital from all the main Wall Street players who had outstanding positions with the nearly insolvent fund. LTCM's partners were rewarded generously for failure. They received double the amount from the bailout than they would have received from the purely commercial offer made earlier by Goldman Sachs and Warren Buffett. The fund was put into administration, and its positions were gradually unwound in an orderly fashion. The terms of this administration allowed the fund to recover and pay to its principals and managers unpaid fees that had been accrued prior to the collapse. Within a year, LTCM founder John Meriwether was running another multibillion-dollar fund.[12]

On February 23, 1990, the United States Government auditor, the General Accounting Office, replied formally to a questionnaire about the LTCM bailout given to them by Senators Byron Dorgan, Harry Reid, and Tom Harkin. In reply to the question, "Did the Federal Reserve's intervention create new incentives for other large financial institutions to take huge financial market risks in the future?" the GAO stated: "...the Federal Reserve Board's intervention probably affected the outcome in this case, and over time such actions could increase moral hazard and potentially undermine the effectiveness of market discipline." Question 12 asked: "Did the Federal Reserve's intervention in LTCM expose American taxpayers to the threat of future hedge fund bailouts?" The GAO replied: "...if companies believe that the federal safety net has been expanded, it may encourage more risky business practices. Based on the LTCM experience, if problems surface during periods of market turmoil, regulators may decide that some form of federal intervention, albeit nonfinancial, may again be necessary."[13]

Greenspan's decision to step in and support Long-Term Capital Management, on terms far more generous than the market was prepared to provide, with no penalty for failure to the people who ran the fund, marked a key turning point in the attitudes to risk taken by market players. For a long time before LTCM, nothing had been considered too big to fail, and plenty did fail, because the dangers of intervening to prevent failure were well known. After LTCM, the market believed that if you got into trouble and you were big enough, the government would rescue you. The belief even got its own name: "the Greenspan put." A put is an option to sell, so what "the Greenspan put" meant was that the market always had an option to sell a problem to the Federal Reserve, at a nice profit. The perception of traders and investors became warped. Attitudes to risk-taking changed, because the odds had become unbalanced. The market became distorted. When Greenspan decided to save Long-Term Capital Management, he intervened in a vital market process—that of failure. If financial entities can't fail, then everything succeeds, for a time. Then everything fails.

At the same time as it organized the orderly wind-down of Long-Term Capital Management, the US central bank lowered rates and added liquidity to the American monetary system in 1998, as a precaution against the system seizing up, to persuade banks to go on lending and consumers to go on borrowing and spending. The consequence of this liquidity surge was the dot-com boom of 1998 to 2000, and it was aggravated by Greenspan's further liquidity additions in the run-up to midnight on January 1, 2000. It was widely believed that older computer software which controlled all public utilities—including power stations, buildings, and traffic lights—would not recognize the change in the "big number" as 1999 became 2000. This, if it happened, could cause chaos throughout developed countries as traffic lights, warning systems, and utilities failed en masse at midnight at the turn of the year 2000.

Although the feared breakdown did not happen, the extra money provided by the Federal Reserve was still there in January 2000. Markets continued to soar until March, when the Federal Reserve started to withdraw the liquidity it had injected, and markets started to fall. The dot-com boom and bust was not real but highly artificial, caused by the Federal Reserve's interference with the market's mechanisms. On the way up, it served to enrich a number of entrepreneurs and early-stage investors who cashed out from stock offerings on the US growth market NASDAQ or from merger deals using inflated stock values, such as AOL's acquisition of Time-Warner. On the way down, it impoverished many investors who had bought towards the end of the boom. It reinforced the belief that the American authorities would intervene in market mechanisms. This belief underlay the increasingly reckless behavior which caused the financial crisis.

After a year of the slowdown induced by the end of the dot-com boom, Greenspan started to worry that demand was stuck in a trough. He had noticed that consumer prices were not rising—many in fact were falling. The prior 10-year average of American consumer price inflation in 1990 was 4.5 percent. In 1995 it was 3.4 percent. By 2001 the prior 10-year average had fallen to 2.5 percent, with consumer price inflation for the year 2001 falling as low as 1.6 percent.[14] Ever-lower consumer prices could be a case for worry, if it meant that households would delay their spending because they thought that they would be able to buy something cheaper in the future.

The Specter of Deflation

At a speech at the Economic Club of New York on December 20, 2002, Greenspan dwelt for some time on the subject of deflation: "It now appears that we have learned that deflation as well as inflation are in the long run monetary phenomena," he said. "Although the US economy has largely escaped any deflation since World War II, there are some well-founded reasons to presume that deflation is more of a threat to economic growth than inflation."[15]

In a deflationary situation, he said, a central bank has somewhat more difficulty in responding, because it is impossible to reduce interest rates below zero. In both his discussion of deflation and his cautious assessment of the economic outlook, Greenspan reinforced the impression among many economists that the Fed did not plan to tighten monetary policy soon.

In the month before Greenspan's speech about deflation, on November 21, 2002, newly appointed Federal Reserve Governor Ben Bernanke had made a speech to the National Economists Club in Washington DC, entitled "Deflation: Making sure 'It' Doesn't Happen Here."[16] The speech was based on work that Bernanke had done while a professor at Princeton. In 1999, he had summarized his research in a co-written paper extolling the virtues of "flexible" inflation targeting, by which he meant that monetary policy operated by central banks, such as the Federal Reserve, should pay as much attention to the risks of deflation as inflation. He pointed out that, even when interest rates were at zero and could fall no further, it was always possible to counter falling prices by printing money. The paper concluded that it was not necessary to worry about asset price bubbles, as long as central banks were obviously committed to price stability. Greenspan's speech a month later appears to show that he had taken Bernanke's clearly expressed views to heart. In 2002 and 2003, the Federal Reserve's low interest rate, expansionary money policy reflected its concern with deflation. Greenspan never made any attempt to curtail the asset price bubble that built up in America after 2002, although he was often asked to do so.

Already through 1998 and 1999 the Federal Reserve had stoked up liquidity. Now it added more fuel, by keeping interest rates low and encouraging bank lending to stimulate consumers after the dot-com bubble burst in 2000. Credit soared, and growth started to pick up strongly. China's supply shock ensured that inflation did not increase in line with demand and money growth, but stayed dormant. Interest rates were kept low until late in 2003. When Greenspan decided at last to normalize them, he used quarter-point increases in small steps over two years to get rates back up to five percent. But by then the damage had been done. The party was out of control.

Repeal of the Glass-Steagall Act

Another key precondition for the financial crisis of 2008 was Wall Street's influence over the American political process in Washington, achieved partly by the huge political lobbying industry, in which America's financial institutions were the biggest players, and partly by the interchange of key personnel between the United States Government and Wall Street. America's investment banks prospered hugely from the economic boom of the 1990s, becoming by the end of the decade many times larger than they had been at the beginning. Years of economic success strengthened Wall Street's hold over the politicians, who benefited greatly from Wall Street's lucrative directorships and advisory contracts. So when the financial sector wanted to change the rules, it was quite easy to get the support of the President.

The rule that the financial institutions wanted to change concerned the separation of the two different kinds of banking. Commercial banks did one kind of banking by taking deposits from the public and lending these customer deposits, plus their own capital, to worthy borrowers. Investment banks did the second kind of banking, which carried much greater potential profit and risk, by using their capital to speculate on their own account. The Depression of 1929 had made both politicians and bankers aware of the potential for economic volatility and bust created when banks could combine both types of banking and were able to speculate in the markets using customer deposits as capital. After the failure of many small banks and the sudden penury of many households who had deposited their savings with them, the *Banking Act of 1933* (the Glass-Steagall Act) aimed to prevent customer deposits from being placed at risk in the market for the benefit of the bank owners and senior managers by making it illegal for a bank to conduct both kinds of banking activity. But in 1999 President Bill Clinton, following a blizzard of lobbying by the American banking industry, was persuaded to repeal part of the 1933 Banking Act, thereby once again permitting banks to draw in customer deposits which they could use as speculative capital on their own account.

At one stroke the repeal of the Glass-Steagall Act vastly increased the capital available to American banks for own-account trading, thereby greatly increasing the possibility of high market volatility and creating the potential for capital losses large enough to wipe banks out, should management oversight fail to stem risk-taking sufficiently. The relatively good performance through the 2008 financial crisis of JP Morgan, a deposit-taking bank with its own proprietary trading, demonstrates that the repeal of the Glass-Steagall Act in 1999 did not necessarily create financial havoc where effective and disciplined management held sway over the blind pursuit of profit. But where the pursuit of profit came before risk oversight, for example in the case of Bear Stearns and Merrill Lynch, huge problems were created both for the banks and for the financial system.

Securitization

Since the 1970s, banks have developed techniques for leveraging their capital by using debt, thereby generating much higher returns to equity. The most important technique was known as structured finance, and the process that led to it was called securitization, which simply meant creating securities, packaging them for sale, and selling them to investors as quickly as possible. To create a security, you needed legal title to an asset that generated regular cash flows, such as a mortgage or a credit card. Bundling lots of income-generating assets together into one security created economies of scale for the banks handling them, and made them more attractive to buyers through diversification. This improved the security's return for a given level of risk. Banks profited twice from creating and selling securities: once on the margin between what they had paid for the assets and what they sold them for as a bundle; and again on the one-off sales commission or spread which was charged on the sales price to the investor who bought the bundle. The other fee earners from securitization were the lawyers who created the securities, and the rating agencies who gave the securities their stamp of approval, or credit rating.

Securitization took off in American banking in the 1980s. It worked well in greatly increasing the amount of risk that could be managed by splitting it up, pricing it accurately, and spreading it among a wide range of investors, and it created an important new source of income for banks. Because the banks were packaging the securities for sale, most of the securitized assets did not show up on banks' balance sheets until the market dried up in 2007 and the securities had to be reclassified as longer term holdings. Handled sensibly, securitization was beneficial and, overall, did more to reduce risk than increase it. But it was possible to introduce the huge, seductive, and dangerous power of leverage by inserting debt in the security alongside the asset. Leverage spiced up the security's return, making it more attractive to yield-hungry investors. Of course, it spiced up the risk as well, because if the interest on the debt wasn't met by the security's inflows, the security rapidly lost value. If a mortgage borrower stopped the monthly payments, the lender would normally try to accommodate these shortfalls until normal payments resumed. But when a bank securitized and sold assets, the bank parted company with the original borrower. Securitization broke the link between original borrower and original lender, making it much harder, or impossible, for the new owners of bank mortgages to manage repayment breakdowns. When banks started lending to less creditworthy (or sub-prime) borrowers and the pattern of mortgage repayments became much more uncertain and breakdowns more common, the loss of the original borrower–lender relationship made attempts to salvage bad loans impossible. Securitization was a great way for banks, lawyers, and rating agencies to raise income and bonuses. It was like a gun, which if used carefully brought only useful results, but if handled carelessly or recklessly could kill. Securitization was a weapon ready and waiting for investors searching for yield and the desire to take on more risk.

The search for yield arising from extremely low interest rates brought aggressive bankers together with yield-hungry buyers. The bankers needed a new, big, fee-generating arena to play in. The American real estate market provided such an arena. American bankers targeted the real estate market for securitization because it was huge and because it seemed low risk. The government mortgage agencies, Fannie Mae and Freddie Mac, had become powerful supports and drivers of the sub-prime mortgage market. Alan Greenspan's testimony before the House Oversight Committee on October 23, 2008, summarized the position well: "It became clear to me in early 2006 that we were in some kind of housing bubble. However, I did not foresee a decline in housing prices because we'd never had one."[17]

Unlike the British, Americans traditionally looked for their stock retirement plans, not their homes, to provide them with capital gain and retirement security. Bringing securitization to American real estate had the great advantage that, as real estate prices had historically neither risen very sharply nor fallen very much, the market was perceived as safe. This made it ripe for securitization and leveraging with debt. In addition, the American Government was keen to encourage home ownership.

China's supply shock kept price increases modest. Central banks accustomed to monitoring consumer price inflation saw nothing to worry about. The recycling of China's growing dollar surpluses back into the American debt markets swelled bank balance sheets and stimulated investors' frenzied search for more risk and higher yields. Three factors, all endemic to the system, combined to make the once-solid American financial system susceptible to collapse: first, a religious belief in free markets which stimulated ever-lighter regulatory oversight; second, an understanding that big organizations who got into trouble would not be allowed to fail; and third, the granting of a license by the repeal of the 1933 Banking Act to banks to bet with their customers' money. Securitization provided the weapon. Cheap credit, fuelled by ultra-low interest rates, years of an easy money policy, and the removal of bank leverage limits in 2005 provided the ammunition. The period of low inflation and high growth—known as "The Great Moderation" and which lasted from 2001 to 2006—caused the markets to start believing that the world really had found the Holy Grail of non-inflationary growth. Thanks to globalization, in particular to the impact of China's economy on the West, it seemed at the time that inflation was dead, and growth could go on forever.

Central bankers, whose job it is to keep our financial system on the rails, did not do much to disabuse onlookers of the notion that things had become permanently better, and that much riskier behavior was fine. The closest to a warning any senior regulator came was a speech given in December 2006 by the deputy governor of the Bank of England, Sir John Gieve, entitled "Pricing for Perfection." Sir John felt there was something wrong, but he couldn't put his finger on it. He ended his speech thus:

Volatility is low, and as time passes, longer memories are needed to remember when it was high. While there have certainly been improvements in macro performance in recent years, I do not know a central banker who is not surprised at the faith that markets appear to have in us to keep the great stability going. And the risks in the wider environment are as great as ever. It is not clear to me that these risks are fully priced into the market. Market forces may not have been able to correct any excess optimism, given the incentives and constraints of participants operating in a world with a good deal of opaqueness about risk-taking.[18]

If the extent of China's impact on the world economy had been better understood at the time, Sir John's instinct, which told him that trouble lay ahead, would have been much more widely supported. A more restrictive monetary policy, which offered greater attractions to savers and smaller incentives to borrowers, would have limited the ballooning of debt and the grotesque unbalancing of the global economy which eventually caused the credit crisis. Chapter 5 discusses whether the use of the dollar as the world currency may have aggravated this problem. Speculation could have been reined in, and the lemming-like search for higher yield moderated. The blame for the catastrophic breakdown of 2008 lies with central bankers, regulators, and politicians, who misunderstood the underlying dynamics created by China's supply shock and ignored the gross oversupply of liquidity, deceiving themselves into thinking that "the great stability" was their creation, and that they had made a new world which would last forever.

Endnotes

1. "The Great Moderation" is an expression introduced early in the millennium to describe the low inflation and low volatility apparently due to new approaches to economic management.
2. *When Markets Collide*, Mohammed el-Erian, McGraw-Hill, 2008.
3. The data series EIUCOCHNTOT from US Bureau of Labor Statistics measures monthly changes in the prices of US imports. It only starts in December 2003. It shows a price fall every year and in most months to October 2006, when prices start to rise again, only getting back to their level of December 2003 by January 2008. The effect of falling import prices on the US, before December 2003, was probably even stronger.
4. See the speech given by Charles Bean, Chief Economist of the Bank of England, "Globalisation and Inflation," to the London School of Economics on October 24, 2006: "...the effect has been to lower the ratios of unskilled labour to skilled labour, as well as driving up the rate of profit on capital...we should expect to see the production of goods and services that are intensive in the use of unskilled labour shifting to

these emerging economies... that is indeed pretty much what has been happening... for much of the past decade, goods price inflation was depressed by the increased availability of cheap imports, especially from Asia." But in March 2007 Ben Bernanke claimed in a speech at Stanford University that Chinese imports had produced an annual negative impact on US inflation of only 0.1 percent. This is probably an underestimate. Also see "China's Trade and Growth: Impact on selected OECD countries," OECD Trade Policy Working Paper no. 44, November 28, 2006.

5. International Labor Organization. The ILO European consumer price series is interrupted by the euro conversion of 1999.

6. See testimony of Treasury Secretary John Snow before the Senate Committee on Banking, Housing and Urban Affairs, October 30, 2003.

7. "A Weakening of the West," Roger Altman, *Foreign Affairs*, January/February 2009.

8. Speech to Labour Party Annual Conference October 2008, quoted in *The Guardian*.

9. "Raw Materials Prices, Wages and Profitability in China's Industry—how was profitability maintained when input prices and wages increased so fast?" World Bank China Research Paper no. 8, Song Yi-Kim and Louis Kuijs, World Bank, October 2007.

10. "Adam Smith's Market Never Stood Alone," Amartya Sen, *Financial Times*, March 23, 2009.

11. Official record of Dr. Alan Greenspan's testimony to the House of Representatives, Oversight Committee, October 23, 2008.

12. "Too Big to Fail? Long Term Capital Management and the Federal Reserve," by Kevin Dowd, Cato Institute Briefing Paper, September 23, 1999. This excellent and far-sighted analysis provides the detailed picture behind the run-up and debacle of LTCM. See also Risk Institute, "Lessons from the Collapse of Hedge Fund Long Term Capital Management" by David Shirreff.

13. "Responses to Questions Related to Long Term Capital Management and Related Events," letter ref. B-284348 by United States General Accounting Office.

14. CPI data series CUSR0000SA0, US Bureau of Labor Statistics.

15. "Greenspan's Speech Focuses on Deflation, not Inflation," Edmund L Andrews, *New York Times*, December 20, 2002.

16. "Deflation: Making Sure 'It' Doesn't Happen Here," remarks by Governor Ben Bernanke before the National Economists Club, Washington DC, November 21, 2002.
17. Official record of Dr. Alan Greenspan's testimony to the House of Representatives, Oversight Committee, October 23, 2008.
18. "Pricing for Perfection," speech by Sir John Gieve at the Bank of England, December 14, 2006.

CHAPTER

3

The Economic Effects of the Crisis on China

The first part of the 2008 crisis happened in the financial world. Protected by a controlled currency, a highly regulated financial sector, and a recently restructured and extremely well-capitalized banking system, China was not much affected by the financial shockwave which flowed from the United States across the Pacific. But the impact of the US banking collapse on corporate activity and consumer confidence created another shockwave, which followed hard behind the first, pushing the developed world into economic recession. As one of the world's largest international trading economies, this shockwave was bound to affect China. Although the government was quick to take preemptive action, China's exports were hit hard by the sharp reduction in consumer demand in the US and Europe which followed the Western banking crisis. This negative economic impact has had two important consequences for China. The first is a realization that a dependence for a large part of Chinese growth on household demand in foreign developed countries is unsustainable. That economic strategy has served China well, but now it has to change. Already the signs of a change of focus in China's economic management are evident. The second consequence is that China knows now that it cannot hide any longer behind the old global power structure which was led by the United States. China's growing economic weight and its more assured posture are having an impact within the Asian region and the world. These realizations, promoted by the crisis, are already having very important results for China and the rest of the world.

In 1976 I was a British soldier based with my infantry regiment in Hong Kong, a tiny British colony on the edge of a huge China still caught in the throes of the Cultural Revolution. Our main job was to patrol the border between British Hong Kong and communist China, which then, as now, ran from Lok Ma Chau in the West across some very steep hills, to end in what then was another fishing village in the East, called Sha Tau Kok. Our purpose was to observe the Chinese on the other side of the border, and capture and return illegal Chinese immigrants to China. From our elevated observation posts, we could see the small villages that lay along the Chinese side of the border, and watch the lives of the Chinese. Their border garrisons were woken at 5.30 a.m. with loud martial music and spent their day marching, studying, and tending plots of vegetables, interspersed with broadcast speeches so loud that we could clearly hear them more than a mile away. Most days we used to bring the Chinese mainland immigrants we had intercepted on the Hong Kong side of the border in a lorry to the border crossing, where we would send them by foot across a bridge, to be greeted on the Chinese side with blows and insults. Today, you can travel on the Hong Kong Metro from Hong Kong Island all the way to the Chinese border at Lo Wu, where the Chinese railway system used to end, and where we once used to exchange curious stares with Chinese guards. Now you can cross the border by foot or car, and catch a train or fly from Shenzhen airport to anywhere in China.

It seems incredible, as we consider China's emergence and new role of world leadership, that it was only three decades ago that China's nightmare of terror was coming to an end, with the imprisonment of the Gang of Four, led by Mao's wife Jiang Qing, followed by the decision by China's leaders to end China's isolation and open the economy to outside influences. The growth story since then, which has taken China's economy ahead of Britain's, France's, and even Germany's to become the world's third largest, may blind us to the fact that China remains in 2009 a very underdeveloped country, with a highly unbalanced economy and a rural population larger and much poorer than the combined populations of Western Europe and America. Analyzing and understanding the effect of the crisis on China, and how it will shape and drive China's and the world's economy and society in the future, requires some consideration of how China got from the time of Mao's death only 34 years ago to where it is now.

In the mid-1700s, when the English diarist James Boswell told his friend, the famous Dr. Samuel Johnson, that he had just been to church and heard a woman preaching the sermon, Dr. Johnson replied that "a woman's preaching is like a dog's walking on his hind legs. It is not done well; but you are surprised to find it done at all." So it was with the first 20 years of China's development following Mao's death. Communist China started to wriggle free from its self-imposed shackles in 1978, the year after the imprisonment of the Gang of Four, when Deng allowed foreign companies to establish joint ventures with Chinese companies and turned a blind eye to starving farmers in Anhui province, west of Shanghai, as they left the commune and started growing their own produce. The first of the foreign companies to enter China was Swiss elevator company Schindler, which established the China Schindler Elevator Company in Beijing in 1980. In the same year Deng initiated the opening of the first four special, and now-famous, economic zones in China's southern coastal provinces of Guangzhou and Fujian, near Hong Kong.

China Takes Off

The spurt of growth that followed in China from these dramatic first steps immediately attracted attention. According to data provided by China's National Statistics Bureau, and measured in local currency terms, from 1980 to 1995 China's economy grew by 12.7 times. Allowing for the more than halving in value of the Chinese currency against the dollar over this period, China's growth was much less, between five and six times. But whichever way you look at it, even allowing for currency changes and measurement inaccuracies (China's triennial national census, which significantly improved data quality, only started in 1995), China was taking off.

But in spite of the spectacular growth numbers and evidence of economic dynamism as cities sprang up in China's coastal areas, it is easy to see why, even in the mid-1990s, most foreign onlookers and economists found it hard to take China's future prospects seriously as a major Asian power, let alone a sustainable economy. China's spectacular growth numbers from the 1980s and early 1990s hid the reality that the same old economy was just running faster and faster, giving rise to the suspicion that soon it would blow up, with nasty and destructive consequences. Nothing fundamental within the machinery of China's economy had changed. The State continued to control every aspect of economic life, setting prices and publishing five-year plans which were financed by State-controlled banks who issued State-printed money to State-controlled companies, whose main task was to employ as many people as possible to produce a predetermined quantity of low-quality, often unwanted products. The politically powerful Chinese army continued to play the major economic role they had under Mao, owning property, operating large factories, and using their power to interfere in every important aspect of economic life. Outside the few coastal special economic zones, where annual growth ran year after year at double-digit rates, foreign involvement in the economy was carefully controlled, being limited to minority stakes in joint ventures with Chinese State-owned companies. The availability of foreign goods in China was restricted by high import duties as well as quotas and other less obvious barriers such as arbitrary quality requirements. In the mid-1990s, Procter and Gamble, the American consumer products company, already betting on China's future, was forced to use the Chinese army to distribute its products throughout China from their production facilities near Hong Kong. Only army trucks could get past Chinese provincial border guards and officials, who would otherwise stop potentially competitive imports from entering their territory from another province unless they were paid a substantial bribe, and even then maybe not.

Without fundamental reform involving some very big structural changes, the only way to stop the centrally planned Chinese economy from overheating was to turn it off, let it cool down, and then restart it, resulting in short cycles of high growth, runaway inflation, and sudden slowdown. One of the causes underlying the unrest in 1989 which ended tragically in Tiananmen Square was the high annual price inflation of over 20 percent which had emerged as Chinese demand—stimulated by increases in employment, wages, and the availability and variety of everyday products—quickly started to outstrip limited supply. Although Deng was able, by his personal example, to persuade the Beijing bureaucrats to restart the economy in 1991, by 1994 inflation was running again at very high rates for the same reason as before: increasing demand which was outstripping the capacity of the economy to meet it.

When Deng Xiaoping, the architect of China's dramatic turnaround, died in 1994, the mourning which gripped the whole country derived partly from a big uncertainty about the future. Who would take the lead now that Deng was gone? But whatever Deng said on his deathbed in 1994 to his successor Jiang Zemin, it seemed to work. The enormous changes that occurred in the six-year period which followed Deng's death laid the foundation of China's prosperity today. By 1995 President Jiang felt strong enough to push aside the old guard of communist conservatives, led by Zhou Enlai's illegitimate son Li Peng, to appoint a new man with new ideas as Prime Minister—Zhu Rongji. The fact that Zhu Rongji had earlier succeeded Jiang Zemin as Mayor of Shanghai may be the key to his appointment and the trust that Jiang showed in him as a reformer. Zhu took immediate action to reduce inflation by the most direct means possible: he ordered the banks, on pain of death, to stop making credit available. By 1996, bank credit had disappeared, inflation had fallen to under eight percent, and the growth rate was plummeting.

Over the next couple of years Zhu, backed by Jiang, got under the hood of China's economy, changing the engine's layout and the working parts. Zhu was not afraid to make the big, fundamental, wrenching changes that China desperately needed. In 1996, to a chorus of complaints and criticism, and steeling himself to a massive potential increase in unemployment amongst the middle-aged, most of whom would never be employed again, he ordered fundamental reform, switching the focus of China's State companies from providing mass employment to improving efficiency, with profitability, not output, as the measure. In 1998 President Jiang, as head of the Chinese Military Commission, forced the Chinese army to sell its businesses and property to focus on becoming an effective national defense force. In the same year, the government's recognition of leasehold ownership rights allowed China's banks to start writing mortgages, and created a market in urban property, allowing a massive monetization via China's banking system which has since been a vital domestic economic driver. Even more important, Zhu stopped China's banks from just being cash machines for State-owned companies, and placed them on a path towards effective risk management, with responsibility for their own assets, liabilities, and profits, to become key cogs in the workings of an increasingly marketized Chinese economy. China's ability to resist the huge shockwaves from the American financial crisis has highlighted the importance of the deep banking reforms which Zhu undertook.

China Becomes an Export Machine

But perhaps the most significant of all of Zhu's reforms, which was sparked by his response to the Asian crisis in 1997, has been overlooked. Zhu reshaped the Chinese economy as an export machine, creating the platform for China's fast growth after the end of the Asian crisis and the 2003 SARS epidemic, thereby laying the foundation for China's dramatic re-emergence into the world and the building up of China's huge pile of foreign exchange. The catalyst for Zhu's export focus was the onslaught of the Asian crisis on China.

In 1997, when the Asian crisis struck, China was reeling under the impact of the restructuring of the State-owned sector. Inflation was falling, but so was growth. Thousands of unproductive factories previously operated by local governments had been closed and thousands others merged, producing a wave of mostly middle-aged unemployed estimated at 50 million, as well as huge one-off costs associated with restructuring and closure. An enormous structural change, from a fully planned to an increasingly marketized economy, was in full swing when China's neighbors in Southeast Asia started to succumb, one after another, to attacks on their currencies and stock markets by Western-based financial speculators. Collapses in Asian financial systems brought huge profits to Western hedge funds who had sold short the local currency and local stocks, outgunning by sheer weight of money the frantic efforts of the national central banks to preserve the status quo, and bankrupting one country after another.

In August 1998 it was Hong Kong's turn, as speculators turned Hong Kong's relative openness and financial sophistication against it, selling the Hong Kong currency and driving down stock prices, replicating the strategy they had used very profitably in Thailand, South Korea, and Indonesia. Forcing the Hong Kong currency to devalue and abandon its fixed link to the US dollar would have precipitated the collapse of much of Hong Kong's banking system and its economy. As Hong Kong struggled to keep out the foreign financial invaders, China came to its support. In 1997 Hong Kong had ceased being a British colony, to become part of China. Thereafter China had to support Hong Kong as one of its own provinces, and as an integral part of the Pearl Basin economy which then supplied most of China's growth. China was also anxious to provide an example of the benefits of rejoining the motherland to its errant province Taiwan, with which it planned reunification one day.

Hong Kong's stunning success in repelling the speculative financial attacks from London and New York in September 1998 owed much to China's support and cooperation. This included support from China's large foreign reserves, as well as information supplied to the Hong Kong Monetary Authority by Chinese based in the New York hedge fund community. By the end of September the speculators had retreated, licking their wounds. But China, already on the back foot because of the negative short-term effect of huge structural change, was still left with the problem of how to deal with the economic collapse which had hit Asia, and which looked like spreading from Hong Kong into mainland China.

The Asian crisis which started in 1997 had a similar pattern to the Western credit crisis of 2008. A severe financial crisis in several

Asian economies in 1997 gave way to a complete loss of consumer and investor confidence in the region. The collapse in demand that ensued produced a harsh regional economic recession. China's enormous restructuring program had increased the Chinese economy's dependence for employment and growth on foreign trade and inward capital flows, most of which at this time were still from overseas Chinese investors based in Hong Kong, Taiwan, Singapore, and other Asian economic centers. Around 60 percent of China's foreign trade was with Asia. Hong Kong, Japan, South Korea, and Taiwan were its most important trading partners. The Asian economic crisis presented China's government in 1998 with an acute and immediate economic threat at a time of major economic transition. China's unemployment had soared. Neither the economy, nor its masters, the Chinese Communist Party, could afford a couple of years of deep recession. Growth had to be found somewhere, and in 1998 the only place to find it was by increasing exports to still-booming Western developed countries, particularly to the largest, the United States. One way for China to do this would have been to let the Chinese currency fall in value against its main trading partners, thereby making Chinese exports cheaper and stimulating demand for them. But China had only just finished assisting Hong Kong to defeat currency speculators from Western hedge funds. It decided against depreciating its currency, which would have sent out a signal of weakness, recognizing that this approach could precipitate a round of competitive devaluations within the east Asian region. Other ways had to be found.

To find them, Prime Minister Zhu appointed a former Trade Minister, Wu Yi, an English-speaking Chinese woman with a no-nonsense reputation, as Minister reporting to China's State Council, with special responsibility for boosting China's exports. Wu Yi organized and led a series of trade missions to China's major overseas markets, reorganized the development of China's export sector, and encouraged foreign multinationals to buy from Chinese factories. She created more special economic zones along China's coastline, with zero taxes on profits and trade, and generous financing packages from Chinese banks to attract foreign companies to plug directly into China's huge low-cost labor force by relocating their manufacturing operations to China.

These initiatives, some of which were equivalent to a highly targeted currency depreciation in that they effectively reduced the price of Chinese exports, started to tilt China's growth towards overseas trade. Large Western multinationals established buying offices in Hong Kong, and those that already had buying offices in Hong Kong established buying offices in Shanghai and Guangdong. The new availability of huge Western markets, and a virtually unlimited supply of cheap, diligent labor, brought out the best in China's army of entrepreneurs. In 1998 China's exports totaled US$183.7 billion, hardly increasing over the previous year's total of US$182.8 billion. Two years later exports had risen by 36 percent to US$249 billion. By 2005 they had more than doubled, to US$660 billion, and by 2008 they had nearly doubled again, to US$1.1 trillion.[1] Li and Fung, the largest company in Hong Kong which specializes in assisting American and European multinationals to source products from Asia, saw its profits rise nearly seven times in the 10 years from 1998, from a Hong Kong dollar equivalent of US$59 million in 1998 to US$392 million in 2007.[2] Not only did China's export boom start to tie China and the West more closely to each other, but by 2008 the dollar volume of China's imports and exports, at US$2.6 trillion, demonstrated how important trade had become to a Chinese economy around US$4 trillion in overall size.[3] The spectacular success of the export-oriented policy which Zhu Rongji and Wu Yi had adopted to deal with the Asian crisis skewed the Chinese economy towards exports and foreign demand. China grew faster, but Chinese growth eventually became unbalanced.

The dramatic increase in Chinese exports after 1999 was largely the result of major foreign multinationals buying from Chinese factories. China became a huge manufacturing entrepot, or assembly shop, as multinationals concentrated their labor-intensive operations there, often importing raw materials or components from several different countries into their Chinese factories for final production, packing, and export. After 2000, as foreign companies responded to China's entry into the WTO, a pattern of Chinese trade developed which reflected this entrepot role, whereby China started to run larger and larger trade surpluses with North America and Europe, and larger and larger deficits with its trading partners in Asia, of whom Japan became the biggest.

Companies based in Japan, Korea, and Taiwan became the dominant players in the China-based supply chain. Between 2000 and 2005 Chinese imports of semi-finished products and components from its largest Asian trading partners Japan, South Korea, and Taiwan grew nearly three times to a total of US$252 billion, amounting to 38 percent of total Chinese imports and dwarfing imports of oil from Russia, iron ore from Brazil, copper from Chile, and aircraft from Boeing and Airbus.[4] China's export trade provided employment to millions of factory workers and kept a huge and expanding transport and logistical network in China's coastal regions busy. But while the dollar amounts of China's trade surpluses soared, the economic value added and kept by Chinese factories as a result of this burgeoning export trade was actually quite small, perhaps only five percent of the final product, with the share gained by Chinese workers a fraction of this, because most of the value of the products lay with designs or technology imported from the host country.

Many foreign companies came to southern China to take advantage of China's low labor costs and the tax benefits offered, and then expanded their buying operations as productivity increased. Productivity improvements came from better trained Chinese workers, better working conditions, improving technology, and geographical concentrations of factories around each group of products, so that parts of the same final product came to be produced within a mile or two of each other. This generated continuous improvements to work organization. Such improvements have always produced dramatic cost reductions and quality improvements wherever they have occurred, from the Scottish textile mills of the early 1800s to Henry Ford's Detroit car factories one hundred years later, and China one hundred years after that. A World Bank study by Song-Yi Kim and Louis Kuijs published in October 2007, which examined the effect of rising costs on Chinese industry, found that in spite of large local cost increases in labor and raw materials between 2002 and 2006, Chinese company profitability actually increased.[5] According to Kim and Kuijs, Chinese wage increases each year of between 10 percent and 15 percent were offset by annual labor productivity improvements of over 20 percent. Continual efficiency improvements over the period were also able to offset average annual raw material price increases of 34 percent. Most exporting factories were even able to accommodate the added cost of Chinese labor laws introduced in 2007, which provided basic safeguards to Chinese workers in the form of social security benefits and unemployment protection. These added a further 15 percent cost to the average Chinese worker payroll, but were also absorbed.

Economists dispute the size of the contribution made by foreign trade to China's growth. Some cite the 40 percent share of the Chinese economy taken up by exports as evidence of their critical importance to growth. Others point to the relatively small share of around five percent occupied by the trade surplus (exports minus imports) in China's overall output as evidence of the relative unimportance of foreign trade, emphasizing instead the roles of household spending and investment as the two main pillars of the Chinese economy. Up until 2008, about 50 percent of China's national output was accounted for by the seven Chinese coastal provinces (Guangdong, Fujian, Zhejiang, Jiangsu, Shandong, Hebei, and Liaoning) and two very large cities (Shanghai and Tianjin). These seven provinces and two cities also produce more than 80 percent of Chinese exports. The other 50 percent of China's national output was produced by the remaining 20 provinces and two other very large cities of Beijing and Chongqing.[6] Even though standard national accounting rules make China's trade surplus a relatively small part of overall output, a significant part of Chinese domestic economic activity clearly depends on foreign trade. While over half of China's foreign trade has been conducted by foreign multinationals, there is no doubt that exports and imports have played a key role in China's economic growth since 2000. Foreign trade is the lifeblood of small island economies such as Singapore, Hong Kong, and Taiwan, which lack the large domestic market possessed by countries such as America and China. China's overdependence on foreign trade is the result of the underdevelopment of its domestic economy.

When the Western economies, the consumers of most of the exports from China, sailed into a big storm in 2008, it was obvious that the impact of the crisis on American and European households was bound to affect China directly. Reports from the main Chinese exporting provinces of Zhejiang and Guangdong started to emerge in June and

July 2008 of large numbers of factories being closed and exporting companies going under. By the end of July 2008, as many as 60,000 Chinese export-focused companies were rumored to have closed down. China's senior leaders Prime Minister Wen Jiabao and President Hu Jintao reacted quickly. In August 2008, immediately after the end of the Olympic Games, both made trips to China's coastal regions to find out for themselves the extent of the economic damage.[7] By November, China was able to offset the shock from the developed countries with a package of government spending which included sales tax cuts and financial packages aimed at helping China's exporters.

A decade after the effects of the 1997 Asian crisis made China's foreign trade into a big growth engine for China, it is hoped that the impact of the 2008 American economic crisis will reduce China's reliance on trade, eventually making China's domestic sector into a motor of Chinese, Asian, and world growth. At the time of writing, the performance of China's economy in the first three months of 2009 already gives clues to the eventual shape of Chinese demand. Compared with a year earlier, foreign trade (exports and imports combined) fell by nearly a quarter, to reduce the annualized rate of Chinese growth to just over six percent, from a growth rate of nine percent for the whole year in 2008 and 13 percent in 2007.[8] The first-quarter six percent growth rate owed everything to a 25 percent increase in investment, driven by government spending in the west and center of China.

The Effect of China's Savings Rate

For China's leadership, the credit crisis has emphasized the dangers inherent in an economy that depends on foreign demand for growth. In future, we can expect China to focus on measures that boost domestically driven demand. There is a problem with this approach. The rate of saving in China is very high. According to China's own statistics, the average Chinese urban income in 2007 was 13,786 Chinese yuan, of which 3,789 yuan was saved. Even in the countryside, where the average annual income was only 4,140 yuan, about 22 percent was saved. In 2007 the average Chinese cash savings balance was 13,058 yuan, about one year's income.[9] China's household savings rates of 20 to 30 percent contrasts with savings rates of typically between five percent and 10 percent in developed economies (and sometimes much less!). Chinese companies, which have generated huge profits over the last five years, also have big cash balances. China, a very large developing country with its own huge need for capital, lends its savings to the United States and to European countries, which are mature economies with much lower savings rates. So reducing China's savings rate and increasing household spending is not just important for China's own economy. It's also vital for reducing China's large surpluses with the US and Europe. If the Chinese spend more, Chinese imports will increase, and the trade surplus will fall. Getting the Chinese to change their saving habit would have an enormous effect on the world economy by making China into a source of strong, sustained demand—the role that the United States has played for many years. But will this happen?

The answer is that if it does, it will not be quick. Asians are savers by nature, and nowhere is this truer than in poor Chinese rural communities, where household annual income may be no more than US$5,000 but they still manage to save as much as 40 percent of their income.[10] The more income that households save, the weaker the effect of an injection of economic stimulus will be, because a significant part of any monetary stimulus in China ends up in the banking system as a deposit, leaving economic circulation until it re-enters as a loan from the bank who took the deposit. The high savings rate means that monetary easing to stimulate spending has to be more aggressive than it would be otherwise. The banks, which capture almost all China's savings, are the most important source of domestic monetary stimulus. The Chinese Government's fine-tuning of the Chinese economy requires careful monitoring of the rate of bank lending and direct control of the amount of lending the banks can make.

The Chinese themselves have seen the savings issue as a key one. Since 2005, the Chinese Government has made great efforts to stimulate consumption and lower the savings rate, but with limited success so far. Measures taken in China's stimulus package late in 2008 aimed at directly encouraging spending included raising wages for 12 million primary and secondary school teachers to the same level as public officials, increasing pensions paid to retired State company employees by 10 percent, and reducing the sales tax on smaller vehicles by 50 percent.[11] Nevertheless, the Chinese savings rate has so far resisted the efforts of the Chinese Government to reduce it. There is some doubt and uncertainty around the reasons for such high Chinese saving, and whether the government really can persuade the Chinese to save less.

In February 2009 a speech by China's central bank governor Zhou Xiaochuan, which focused on the issue of high Chinese savings, shed light on China's approach to the saving issue.[12] The governor attributed the characteristic Asian desire to save to several factors. One was a Confucian culture of non-extravagance. Another was the desire of Asian families to be independent, and to look after their old and young dependents themselves. A third explanation he gave was that high economic growth rates, which generated high employment, encouraged in turn a high level of personal saving. Zhou did not accept the commonly held view that a large part of Chinese savings are precautionary, held to fund unexpected hospital bills or a forced early retirement in the absence of nationwide pension and healthcare schemes. He argued that this conclusion assumed a level of rationality on behalf of Chinese consumers which the on-the-ground evidence did not support. Zhou noted that the largest part of Chinese savings are company savings, which he explained as a consequence of the reform of the Chinese State sector in 1996 and 1997. This reform took away the responsibility on State companies to provide cradle-to-grave care for their workers. Companies had been slow in adjusting previously low workers' salaries up to levels which were competitive with privately owned companies. For a decade or so, Chinese State companies enjoyed a cost subsidy from low employee wages. This period allowed them to build up large surpluses. In his view, this partly explains the high level of China's reserves. He also rejected as unproven the link between China's build up of reserves and the undervaluing of its exchange rate, which has been a central assumption of American policy toward China in recent years.

China has three characteristics that make for a naturally high saving rate. One is that it is only three decades since a period of dreadful poverty and hardship in China. A Chinese person born in 1945, now in his or her mid-60s, would have been of young working age at the beginning of China's appalling Cultural Revolution in 1966, and can easily remember a long period of great hardship and difficulty. Although in 2009 it has become more unlikely that circumstances in China might return to those conditions, the many ups and downs of Chinese history argue for a cautious approach. Another is that, although China's leaders may meet on equal terms the leaders of the most powerful countries in the world, the country's huge population makes it still a poor country. On a per capita basis, China's savings are a fraction of those held by rich Asian countries such as Japan, Hong Kong, Taiwan, Singapore, and South Korea. It will be many years before the majority of China's population can be counted as reasonably affluent.

The third, most significant, factor is that, while China is much poorer than most of its Asian neighbors, the country's population is aging faster than many of them. A large future increase in the number of retired people suggests a building up of savings now to be drawn down in a few years when the average age starts to shift away from the working towards the retired population. The most recent estimates at the time of writing (from an April 2009 paper published jointly by the Center for Strategic and International Studies based in Washington DC, and the Prudential Foundation) show that in the 10 years from 2010, for the first time, China's working population will not increase, while the over-60 retired population will grow by an estimated 74 million.[13] In the following decade, between 2020 and 2030, China's working population will actually shrink by 65 million, while the Chinese over-60s will increase in number by 105 million. While China's falling fertility rates and higher life expectancies apply also to many other countries, both developing and developed, two China-specific factors aggravate China's aging problem: the one-child policy adopted in the 1980s, and the traditional Chinese preference for boys, who provide an extra pair of hands on the farm or in the factory, over girls, who have little or no economic benefit. This preference for male children distorts the standard global 106:100 boy:girl ratio at birth to a ratio observed in China in 2005 of 119 boys to 100 girls. This view gains support from work done by UBS bank economist Jonathan Anderson and described by George Magnus in his recent book *The Age of Aging*.[14] Magnus notes that the improvement in China's demographic profile between 1980 and 2003 accounted for about one-quarter of the considerable gain in per capita Chinese income over that time. But he estimates that any benefit which has occurred from China's demographics will disappear around 2015, and from that time Chinese savings will start to fall as they are drawn down to meet medical expenses and retirement benefits. At least half of China's huge savings belong to State-owned enterprises, arising largely from the restructuring of the Chinese State sector a decade ago which removed social security obligations. It would be both fair and possible for the Chinese Government to tax company savings to fund the increased social security demands being made upon it. Meanwhile most Chinese workers will still be too poor to be in a position to save enough while simultaneously increasing their spending. In 1996 the Chinese National People's Congress passed a law obliging children to support their aging parents. Especially in the countryside, many retired people, and most of the over-80s, are supported by their younger relatives. In 2008, 69 percent of China's population was not covered by a retirement plan.[15] So the future drawdown of savings called for by China's demographic maturity will probably be the result of government-led dissaving, rather than a big change in Chinese consumer behavior.

It is difficult to escape the conclusion that the Chinese household savings rate is not going to fall very much, if at all, for some years at least, although consumption may start to increase somewhat as the demographics start to shift significantly toward the retired population from around 2015. China needs to use its savings more efficiently and productively, and China's own capital markets need to get much better at transferring surplus capital from Chinese savers to the companies and households who can use it to expand their businesses or enlarge their lifestyles. China's capital markets remain very undeveloped, and their ability to intermediate between savers on the one hand and users or investors of capital on the other remains weak, with banks still carrying out most of this function. Although returns on bank deposits are kept low by a Chinese Government anxious to support bank profitability, as at mid-2008 bank deposits in China outweighed money invested in stocks by 8 to 1.[16] Although bond and stock markets in China have grown enormously since their beginnings in the early 1990s, according to figures supplied by the China Banking Regulatory Commission more than 80 percent of China's corporate financing is still supplied by bank loans, with only about 10 percent coming from corporate bonds and four percent from equities or stocks. Of the bonds issued, more than half have maturities of one year or less. China's banks have improved out of all recognition since their reforms a decade ago, but the operation of China's stock markets is still dominated by cautious regulators, while Chinese domestic money markets and corporate bond markets remain rudimentary. Important steps have been taken in recent years, including the confirmation of private property rights in 2004, the conversion of State-owned shares to tradable shares in 2005, and the liberalization of corporate bond markets in 2007. And as a part of the stimulus plan announced at the end of 2008, China has recently allowed local governments to start raising their own funds, by issuing bonds against the credit of the Ministry of Finance in Beijing. But there is still a long way to go before even a quarter of China's population become as familiar with spending and investing as they are with saving.

China's Current Account Surpluses

If China's savings rates remain high, as they look like doing, China's current account surpluses could persist for some years to come, and China's foreign reserves, which at the last count totaled just short of US$2 trillion, could continue to grow. Compared with a year ago, in the first three months of 2009 trade fell by a quarter, but the surplus of exports over imports rose to US$62.3 billion, an increase over the previous year of US$20 billion. This is in line with a pattern of continued high savings. Even allowing for a bounce back in domestic demand once confidence returns in China later in 2009, if the saving rate stays high, China's foreign reserves could easily double or more from their current levels of around US$2 trillion, before a peak is reached, and the country starts to draw down its savings as its working population starts to shrink. By comparison on a per capita basis, a trebling of China's foreign reserves from the current level would bring China roughly in line with South Korea's level of reserves, but that would still represent only half the current Japanese level of savings per head.

The difficulty of changing China's growth model could mean that exports will continue to play an important role in China's economic growth for some years to come, and that the central bank will continue to manage the level of the Chinese yuan against the currencies of its main trading partners, particularly the dollar. Even though China may allow full convertibility of its currency into other currencies for all transactions quite soon, the destruction wrought in Asian economies in 1997–98 by foreign investors will continue to make China wary of allowing free trading of its currency. Nevertheless, if domestic Chinese consumption fails to compensate for reduced Chinese exports, China will have to fall back on government spending to grow its economy, something that comes much more naturally to a centrally planned economy such as China than it does to the United States. If private citizens will not or cannot spend, then the government has to take up the slack and spend money on their behalf. China's central planning tradition has endowed it with a powerful bureaucratic apparatus for organizing large-scale budgets and spending organized through the 31 provincial and large city governments and the county governments in each province, with further local spending to be financed by provincial bond issues. No large country does this better. China was the first large country to announce a major government-sponsored economic stimulus as the first indications of a major slowdown started to show through in mid-2008. By November 2008, the government had their economic package ready, announcing a spending plan totaling 4,000 billion yuan (about US$600 billion) to be spent over two years. They started to disburse this quickly, with 100 billion yuan (US$15 billion) released by the end of 2008, 130 billion yuan (US$19 billion) in the first three months of 2009, and larger amounts planned for the remaining quarters of 2009.[17] The results started to show through early in 2009, with investment in fixed assets in the first quarter growing at nearly 30 percent over the previous year, amid signs that confidence within China was starting to rise again from lows reached in the early part of 2008. The Development Research Center, a Beijing-based government think tank, estimated in 2009 that

China would spend 5,740 billion yuan (about US$840 billion at the exchange rate at the time of writing) on social welfare by 2020 to extend to its huge population pensions, healthcare, housing, and education.[18] In January 2009, China's State Council agreed to the first installment of this 10-year project, a three-year plan costing 850 billion yuan (about US$124 billion) to bring healthcare coverage to 90 percent of the population. The details released in March included the construction of a clinic in every Chinese village, 2,000 large hospitals at county level, 3,000 community clinics, and 11,000 health centers.[19]

The crisis has forced governments everywhere to carry the burden of investment spending for years to come, while the once-buoyant private sector gets back on its feet. This places huge strains on government finances. China has been able to enter the crisis in clearly the strongest financial position of any major economy. It has the world's largest stock of foreign currency reserves and the fastest growing large economy. Both long- and short-term debt is low, while fast-rising tax revenues produced a budget surplus in 2008. Moreover, a trip around China reveals that spending on roads, railways, bridges, public buildings, and dams—infrastructure of every kind—is badly needed. In China, there is a long way to go before bridges start going to nowhere, as they started to do in the 1990s in Japan, a far smaller country.

China's economic stimulus has been financed by an explosion of bank credit. Worries in 2008 about a Chinese economic implosion following the collapse in Western demand for Chinese exports have been replaced by fears of Chinese asset price bubbles and overheating. While the gap between potential and actual Chinese economic output remains wide enough and the monetary control of the Chinese Government currently remains active enough to allay these fears, there still is an underlying problem here which arises from the lack of Chinese monetary controls. A government can choose to control either the level of its currency's exchange rate, or the level of domestic interest rates, but not both. By fixing the yuan against a basket of major currencies, of which the US dollar is the most important, China has yielded sovereignty over its domestic interest rate policy to the US Federal Reserve. China needs to regain control of its monetary policy, in order to increase the margin of safety around its economic management. This comprises a strong argument for an end to China's fix of the yuan against the currencies of its major importers in the US and Europe, particularly as US interest rates look likely to remain very low for a long time. A genuinely floating Chinese currency would allow the proactive use of Chinese domestic interest rates to ration credit and manage inflationary expectations. This would greatly reduce the likelihood of a Chinese asset price bubble resulting from continued economic stimulus.

But China's budget surplus in 2007 of around three percent of GDP will turn to deficit over the next decade or more as the country becomes the world's second largest spender, after the United States, on public projects such as education, healthcare, national defense, and public infrastructure, including railways, roads, and airports. China's often hostile land is difficult to farm. Its farming sector cannot support many of China's 800 million or more rural residents. A large number of these people will move to new towns built specially for them over the course of the next generation. China will continue to invest for many years to come, to create an urban infrastructure in the center of China which links the poor west of the country with the prosperous east. This involves the planning and building of as many as 500 modern cities to house migrants from the countryside. China is already taking steps to secure the basic mineral resources from around the world that will be needed to create the facilities to house this enormous newly urban population. As in most other large economies, the crisis has pushed China's public finances into deficit. But unlike many other countries, China can easily finance its deficits itself, because its savings pool is so large. In the international arena, this is as great a source of strength to China today as the US's financial strength was to it after the Second World War. China's relatively quick emergence from the crisis, which contrasts with the profound, longer–term debilitating effects of debt reduction on the developed countries, is set to work wonders for the country's position and reputation in the world.

When Hu Jintao became China's President in the spring of 2003, China's reputation was poor. It had already taken a beating as a result of the Tiananmen Square incident in 1989, the country's human rights record, and its relationship with Tibet. Since 1980, China's image of quaintness and exotic Shangri-La mystery, which the

American-educated wife of the Chinese Nationalist leader and wartime ally General Chiang Kai-Shek, had cultivated so successfully in the United States before and during the Second World War was replaced by a picture of a polluted, overpopulated, communist country producing cheap imitations of Western products and holding large numbers of its population in prison camps. As evidence of a SARS cover-up in high places started to leak out shortly after Hu took over, China's reputation for integrity took a further dive. China was aware of its bad public image in many countries, and planned the Beijing Olympic Games in August 2008 to transform the world's perception of China. After seven years of planning and spending US$40 billion, China provided an Opening Ceremony watched by an estimated one billion people around the world. The Beijing Olympics was planned as a coming-out party, but the crisis made it the start of a bigger global emergence than anyone, including the Chinese leadership, could have imagined. The televised pictures at the Olympic Games of George W Bush and other global leaders proceeding, one by one, up a red carpet to shake hands with China's President, who received them at the head of the carpet in the way he might greet loyal tributaries, did raise questions in the minds of some of those watching. But eight months later when the official photograph of the G20 summit in London showed the Chinese President standing at the right hand of British Premier Gordon Brown, no one raised an eyebrow because it seemed a natural recognition of China's role as the country with the cash, the size, and the growth capacity to come to the rescue.

The bankruptcy of Lehman Brothers on September 15, 2008 and the sudden crisis that hit the world's financial markets immediately afterwards thrust China into a new role in the world. The sudden, chronic weakness of the main pillar of the world system, the United States, left a huge power vacuum. A vacuum does not last long in the fast-moving world of nature or in the equally cruel world of international politics. Already China has moved to fill part of the vacuum left by the shrinkage in the reputation of the United States, both in Asia and elsewhere. The focus of the Chinese Government is on looking after the one-fifth of the world's population who live in China. Chinese Government actions are primarily determined by the effect they would have on China's development. But China cannot become a fully developed country on its own. As its economy grows and the country becomes more sophisticated, it increasingly needs the rest of the world. China's leaders recognize this reality and are moving tentatively to a central place in world affairs, one from which they can develop international relationships with other major countries that will serve China well over the longer term. Multilateral institutions are set to assume a new importance in a world no longer dominated by one superpower, the United States.

Endnotes

1. *China Statistical Yearbook* 2008, National Bureau of Statistics of China.
2. Annual accounts 2008, Li and Fung Ltd.
3. International Monetary Fund: Data and Statistics http://www.imf.org, June 2009.
4. *China Statistical Yearbook* 2008, National Bureau of Statistics of China.
5. "Raw Material Prices, Wages and Profitability in China's Industry – how was profitability maintained when input prices and wages increased so fast?" World Bank China Research Paper No 8 by Song-Yi Kim and Luis Kuijs, October 2007.
6. *China Statistical Yearbook* 2008, National Bureau of Statistics of China.
7. *People's Daily*, various reports August and September 2009.
8. *China Statistical Yearbook* 2008, National Bureau of Statistics of China.
9. Ibid.
10. Ibid.
11. *People's Daily*, January 2009.
12. "On Savings Ratio," Zhou Xiaochuan, People's Bank of China Web site, February 2009.
13. "China's Long March to Retirement Reform," Richard Jackson et al., Center for Strategic and International Studies, 2008.
14. *The Age of Aging*, George Magnus, John Wiley & Sons, 2008.
15. "China's Long March to Retirement Reform," Richard Jackson et al., Center for Strategic and International Studies, 2008.
16. "China's Financial Markets—a Future Global Force?" Syetam Hansekul et al., Deutsche Bank Research, March 16, 2009.
17. *People's Daily*, January 2009.
18. *People's Daily*, April 2009.
19. Ibid.

4

From G8 to G20: China's Role in Global Governance

he credit crisis changed the world's view of China, to something like an island appearing over the horizon to a boatload of shipwreck survivors. China's large cash reserves and economic growth made it stand out at a time when developed countries were shrinking and had to borrow heavily to shore up their own crisis-hit economies. There are new expectations of China's role in global governance. And China is showing signs that it is aware of the expectations requiring it to step from behind America's shadow into the limelight. Like a large tree shedding one of its heaviest branches, thereby allowing smaller trees around it to reach up to the sunlight, the weakening of the United States as a result of the 2008 crisis has encouraged changes in the configuration and relative positioning of the major countries in the world. Among the major countries which surround America in the global order, China is in a special position.

Simple mathematics demonstrates that its economy will overtake Japan's in absolute size in two or three years, and America's in between 20 and 30 years from now.

China's Challenge

This challenge comes to China at an early time in its emergence. At home, a great deal remains to be done. Much of China's economy remains immature and undeveloped. For instance, its financial sector is still unable to support much of the economy's development. The government still controls tightly the international use and external value of the Chinese yuan. China houses one of the world's largest populations of poor people, and will continue to do so for many years to come. There is a big difference between absolute economic size on the one hand, and wealth measured by income per household or per head of population on the other. Unlike the G7 countries, which are all rich countries, however measured, China is not at liberty to make gestures or spend resources that do not directly apply to its own problems. This point was well brought out by Chinese Premier Wen Jiabao during his interview in February 2009 with Lionel Barber, the editor of the London-based *Financial Times*:

> **Lionel Barber:** "... for 30 years some people have said capitalism will save China, and now maybe people are saying China must save capitalism."

> **Wen Jiabao:** "Well, I don't see it this way. I still have a very clear mind on this particular point. China remains a big developing country with a 1.3 billion population. We do face arduous tasks, and our way ahead will be a long one. If you have seen the Chinese cities in the coastal areas, maybe you don't see much difference between those cities and London, but if you have ever been to China's rural areas, particularly the western areas of China, you will see a big gap."[1]

The credit crisis has afforded China a broader global role. In pursuing this role, China will be guided by its pressing domestic agenda.

China's relationship to the rest of the world is like a half-grown elephant in Noah's Ark, sharing a confined space with other smaller animals. China, which has not finished growing by any means, cannot advance its own agenda without finding ways to effectively cooperate with other countries. It is for this reason that China must seek to be increasingly involved in every aspect of world governance that affects its own interests. These interests are dominated by the issues of its own sovereignty, particularly those issues involving Taiwan and Tibet, and by opportunities for economic growth which provide employment and basic services to its population.

China's strong-yet-weak international position was well demonstrated in 2002 and 2003, when the United States was looking for international support for its attack on Iraq and the unseating of Saddam Hussein, and when China's export boom to America was at its height. Since the foundation of the UN in 1946, China has been one of the five permanent members of the UN Security Council, with the power to veto any substantive resolution. The permanent membership, like that of the other global multilateral organizations, represents the ultimate in high-level power clubs, reflecting the global status quo at the end of the Second World War, and includes France, Russia, Britain, and the United States in addition to China. Security Council permanent membership is a position that allows China to exercise considerable influence, if it chooses. The UN Security Council, which derives its power from the UN constitution, operates as a global policeman, and has at its disposal an effective force of UN peacekeepers. In November 2002, the then 15 members of the Security Council (of whom 10 were elected and five were permanent members) voted unanimously for Resolution 1441 which delivered an ultimatum to Iraq. This resolution was later relied on by America in March 2003 as a pretext for the declaration of war. Of the three permanent Council members who could have voted down Resolution 1441, China sat on the fence, leaving France and Russia to oppose the United States (and its ally Britain) in persuading the UN that Iraq was a threat to world peace. After the Security Council vote in favor of the American motion, the American ambassador John Negroponte made America's intentions very clear, describing Resolution 1441 in this way:

If the Security Council fails to act decisively in the event of a further Iraqi violation, this resolution does not constrain any member state from acting to defend itself against the threat posed by Iraq, or to enforce relevant UN resolutions and protect world peace and security.[2]

Following inconclusive findings by the UN weapons inspectors, led by Hans Blix, and after France had threatened to veto any Council resolution that led immediately to war with Iraq, in March 2003 America, backed by the British, decided to proceed unilaterally against Iraq.

If the three permanent Security Council members, China, Russia, and France, had acted firmly in unison on their strong suspicion that America was cooking up a case to go to war for private reasons, between them they could have stopped America and Britain from attacking Iraq. But China depended too much on the American market for its exports, which were at that time starting to bring huge inflows of dollars into China's Treasury. China could not risk provoking an American retaliation in 2003, and abstained. France and Russia on their own were not powerful enough to face up to the two other permanent members of the Security Council, Britain and the United States. They had to give way. Although France, to its great credit, promised to veto an invasion, America went ahead anyway, without further referral to the Security Council.

The message from this episode is that, although in the international context China appears increasingly powerful and important, it remains at the mercy of the difficulties it still faces in providing for the needs of its huge population. China, unlike France, cannot afford to support moral causes on the international stage, however important, that could damage its economy.

China's Role in Global Institutions

Although China's leaders would prefer to wait a few more years before taking a leading role, the sudden change in the developed countries' economic and financial circumstances mean that they look to China as a partner now. The question before China is how to exercise its power in the most efficient way, and which global institutions it should focus on. The Chinese are taking steps in various different directions to see which ways work best. For instance, January 2009 saw the first visit by Chinese Premier Wen Jiabao to the Davos World Economic Forum meetings. China's new role is a complex and delicate issue given the historical dominance of the Western developed countries over the global institutions of governance, and given the importance of China gaining power in a peaceful and cooperative way which commands support and does not ruffle feathers. To a large extent, the power transfer concerns the United States, whose superpower status, since 1945, has underpinned the way the world works. No key decision of global significance, be it China joining the WTO in 1999 or the Kyoto climate change agreement which came into force in 2005, has been able to work unless backed by the US, whose dominance over the world's multilateral institutions sprang from its own economic strength and the insolvency of the victorious European countries at the end of the Second World War.

The new global monetary and economic system established at the end of the Second World War was modeled along American lines, in which the US dollar became the world currency. The agreement reached in 1944 at Bretton Woods broke up the pre-war global trading system which had protected France and Britain and their dependencies around the world from American industrial might, with which they could not compete head on. In return for getting the loans they desperately needed, the two old imperial powers agreed to a new economic and financial order with the United States at its head, which opened up their traditionally closed markets. The US dominated the new open economic order, and the institutions established to operate it: the International Monetary Fund (IMF), established as the policeman of the global financial architecture, with the purpose of protecting trade flows between countries and assisting countries in difficulties with their external accounts; and the World Bank (founded as the International Bank for Reconstruction and Development), established to finance desperately needed recovery from the war.

When the first multilateral institutions were established in 1945, the only major country in the world with any significant spending power was the United States. Like Britain, its territory had not been invaded by another power, but unlike Britain it was solvent, with a currency that everyone believed in. American control over the new post-war institutions was necessary to ensure their effectiveness and that the American money that backed them was used in a way which did not conflict with American interests. In return for providing one-third of the capital backing for the IMF and the World Bank, the US secured control by requiring a voting majority of 85 percent of the membership. The US voting share, originally 33 percent, now stands at just 16 over percent, more than twice as much as the next largest world economy, Japan, and three or more times the voting power of each of Germany, France, and Britain. The blocking stake in the IMF and the World Bank which the United States still holds makes it impossible for any other country or group of countries to introduce changes of which the US does not approve. The 11 presidents of the World Bank since foundation have all been American. By mutual agreement with the European powers, the presidents of the IMF have always been European. The IMF and the World Bank both acquired enormous power in the years after the war, because they became the principal organs of financial support for the post-war world. The UN, which was founded a year later in 1946, is the most inclusive of the global multilaterals, with each country getting one vote irrespective of size or power. But its power has always been limited by its dependence on the largest member countries, led by the United States, to meet its annual running costs. Outside the Security Council, the UN has consequently never exercised the same degree of influence as the IMF and the World Bank, who have privileged access to the world's credit markets, making them a major financial force and a vital source of credit support to reconstructing and developing economies.

As the developed world became richer, the world's needs changed. Both the IMF and the World Bank found that, to survive, they had to find new needs and redefine their roles to meet them. In general, this meant switching their focus away from the rich developed world towards emerging countries. The World Bank did better out of these changes than the IMF, because its original remit was more flexible. Its original role of post-war reconstruction gave it relevance to the emerging world, to which its focus switched. Once the United States had stopped fixing its dollar to gold in 1971, and exchange rates had started to float against each other from 1973, the most important part of the IMF's role, of managing a system of fixed exchange rates, disappeared. The organization, originally conceived as the issuer and guardian of a new world currency which never came to pass, struggled to retain its relevance in a world with floating exchange rates and with an American superpower that had become less interested in taking advice from multilateral institutions in which it had to share control. The resurgence of the American economy and increased power of the dollar that followed the collapse of the Soviet Union in the 1980s, and the tremendous growth in international flows of private capital in the 1990s, marginalized the IMF. Meanwhile, the World Bank had to go through its own identity crisis in the 1990s before it became focused on alleviating poverty. The membership of both institutions changed as new economic forces appeared and old ones receded. But as the United States has continued to effectively control both, the other original founders, whose global economic influence has waned, such as Britain, France, and Canada, have been able to hang onto a significant degree of influence, and both institutions have been increasingly criticized for narrowly reflecting the interests of their original shareholders. The United States, Canada, Japan, and the seven leading western Europeans (Germany, the United Kingdom, France, the Netherlands, Spain, Italy, and Belgium) between them control over 50 percent of the votes at both the IMF and the World Bank. Meanwhile the combined voting power at both institutions of the largest emerging countries China, India, Brazil, and Russia stands presently at around 10 percent. China has to consider whether it can ever really bring its influence to bear on these institutions.

Although the multilateral organizations founded at the end of the war provided a full scope for global governance, the United States started to prefer to settle world affairs directly one-to-one as its wealth and influence grew, without the inconvenience and delay, not to mention the possibility of contradiction, brought by involvement with multilateral organizations, such as the UN whose one country, one vote system made it a difficult organization for the Americans to control. The first big global economic crisis since 1945 that required a globally coordinated response was caused by the oil price rises of 1973. This was met by forming a new informal group of the wealthiest large countries, which became known in 1976 as the G7, and in 1997, with the accession of Russia, as the G8. While the memberships of the IMF, the World Bank, and the UN all had claims to universality, the G8, with wealth as the sole membership qualification, had none. The combined G8 membership today reflects high shares of world trade, world economic output, and world oil production, but less than 20 percent of the world's population.[3] In contrast, in 1944 the representatives that had met at Bretton Woods to reorganize the world economy were drawn from all the 44 countries, large and small, who had joined the Anglo–American cause as allies against the Axis countries. Implicit in the formation of the G6/7/8, 30 years after the war was the idea that a small group of the world's richest and most powerful countries could decide important global questions on behalf of all the other countries in the world. This approach worked while the G8 countries, led by the United States, dominated the world economy.

In the 1990s, emerging countries everywhere started to benefit from the growth which followed the collapse of the Soviet Union. The world started to outgrow the G8. The virulence of the Asian economic crisis in 1997 and the Russian debt crisis of 1998 made necessary the creation of a new kind of forum which reached out to emerging countries to create a broader platform from which to discuss major economic problems and decide on solutions. In theory, either of the institutions created at Bretton Woods, the IMF or the World Bank, which both had broad memberships, could have provided such a forum. But in practice both were perceived as being too bureaucratic and specialized to act as a launch pad for an effective global response to the financial crises of the late 1990s. America and the other major nations looked instead for an extension of the G7/8 group, and came up with the G22, which met in Washington DC in April 1998, and again in October, with the purpose of finding a common solution to the Asian crisis. The group was expanded to the G33 in 1999, and then, as this proved too unwieldy, the G20 emerged as a representative grouping of practical size which brought the financial secretaries of emerging and developed countries together in annual meetings. Meanwhile, the G8 continued to meet as the dominant group of rich nations, inviting China, India, Mexico, Brazil, and South Africa in 2003 to join them at their annual meeting at Evian-les-Bains in France, hosted by French President Jacques Chirac. The new grouping was called the G8+5 in an attempt to avoid diluting the exclusivity of the G8 club, while bringing some of the emerging countries inside the tent to provide the G8 with global legitimacy.

When the full force of the credit crisis struck in September 2008, neither of the original multilateral institutions, the IMF and the World Bank, was immediately chosen as the organization to coordinate the response to the crisis. Although the G8 met immediately after the crisis in October 2008, the problem was obviously too wide-reaching for a group that did not include at least China and India. It was the G20 summit held in New York in November that attracted the most attention and support, because for the first time it brought the major emerging countries, led by China, to join the rich countries in search of a world solution to what had become a world problem. The G20 November summit in New York issued a declaration which could purport to be representative of all the major economies in the world, not just North America, Europe, and Japan. It stated:

> *We are determined to enhance our cooperation and work together to restore global growth and achieve needed reforms in the world's financial systems.*[4]

Because America had been stricken by the crisis, a group that included the largest emerging countries as well as the world's major energy supplier Saudi Arabia had become necessary for the first time to work out and execute a response. The G20 went on to confirm the focus on reform of the multilateral institutions:

> *We underscored that the Bretton Woods Institutions must be comprehensively reformed so that they can more adequately reflect changing*

economic weights in the world economy and be more responsive to future
challenges. Emerging and developing economies should have greater
voice and representation in these institutions.[5]

The London G20 summit of April 2009 confirmed that the G20
was looking like becoming the new G8. But Italy and the other smaller
members of the G8, such as Britain, clearly stand to lose influence if
the G20 takes over from the G8 as the global governance grouping of
choice. So China, India, Mexico, Brazil, and South Africa were invited
to attend the G8 meeting in July 2009 hosted by Italy at L'Aquila.
In the words of the Italian Foreign Minister, the Italian-hosted G8
meeting in July is focusing on financial stability and growth "in a spirit
of collaboration and not competition with the G20." But the smaller
G8 grouping lacks legitimacy among the important emerging countries,
led by China. This situation was hinted at in an assessment written
in November 2008 by the chief executive of the IMF, Dominique
Strauss-Kahn, which outlined the actions the London G20 summit in
April 2009 needed to consider:

Forewarned, the world must also be forearmed with a mechanism for
effective action. Many have questioned whether existing groupings,
the various Gs, are sufficiently representative or have the needed
infrastructure for follow up and implementation. There is a need for
a suitably sized and representative group of key policymakers able
to agree on a consistent approach that might frame follow up at the
national and multilateral levels. The IMF is prepared to play its
part in supporting any such initiative to coordinate and monitor policy
responses.

There have been numerous calls in recent months for a "new Bretton
Woods agreement," which I strongly endorse. However, one important
lesson of the original Bretton Woods agreement was that its foundations
were carefully laid through serious and vigorous discussion of the
underlying issues. I therefore very much welcome the initiative taken by

the President of the United States to bring together the G-20 leaders,
to follow up with various working groups, and culminate these efforts in
a conference, hopefully within the year ahead.[6]

The enduring success of the Bretton Woods meeting in 1944, involving representatives from all 44 allies, was partly attributable to its inclusivity. Since then, the gradual emergence of a global status quo based on the military and economic power of the United States—the so-called "Pax Americana," reinforced by the collapse of the Soviet Union in 1989 and the success of the American economy in the 1990s—has made Americans increasingly impatient of globally representative institutions such as the General Assembly of the UN in solving important global economic or security problems. The American lack of regard for the Security Council and the French veto, which was demonstrated in 2003 when American troops attacked Iraq, has undermined the reputation of the US in the Muslim world and much of the rest of Asia. These disastrous results have not been lost on the Chinese, who maintain that an inclusive not exclusive or unilateral approach to solving international problems provides a much better prospect of longer-term success.

The financial crash in September 2008 around the bankruptcy of Lehman Brothers, and the ensuing market panic, made the Chinese leaders realize that, in order to achieve their goal of developing China into a modern, wealthy society, they could not continue to hide behind American dominance. Neither was there anyone else who was big enough to hide behind. They had to go it alone. It was time to emerge into the open. Consequently, since October 2008, China has started to adopt a more independent approach, working with several different institutions, while supporting extensive and fundamental reform of the original Bretton Woods institutions. This approach has started to change global governance. China preferred not to become a regular member of the G8, as it sees this grouping as an exclusive club for rich countries which is controlled by America. Given China's low income per capita, is it appropriate for China to become a junior member of an exclusive club for rich countries? The membership list of a global club organized

by China would look very different from the G8, and would probably
include at the top table with China, other large emerging countries such
as India, Russia, and Brazil. Smaller European countries such as Spain,
Italy, and even Britain and France would probably be seated lower
down with Poland, Saudi Arabia, and South Africa.

Pragmatism is a Chinese virtue, and China has committed itself to
working with things as they are. The question for China is how it
should do this. There are various world multilateral organizations that
have claimed a legitimate interest in coordinating the global response
to the crisis: the G8, which has been the principal world management
forum since the 1970s, but is now unrepresentative of the key large
developing countries such as China; the G20, which has developed as
a G7 or G8 organization but with greater international legitimacy; the
IMF, which was originally established at the Bretton Woods meeting in
1944 as the global multilateral organization to manage the international
financial system; the IMF's sister organization the World Bank; and
the UN, which as a G192 organization claims the greatest legitimacy
of all. For China, the influence and international legitimacy that an
organization wields, as well as its flexibility, are the important factors
in deciding which one it should throw its weight behind. In 2006,
the IMF was the first organization to start reforming itself in response
to the changes in the distribution of economic power and influence
in the world. In April 2008, it voted overwhelmingly to adjust the
voting rights of its membership, by taking a total of 5.4 percent of
the voting power from Britain, France, and other mostly developed
countries and giving it to a group of mostly emerging countries led
by China. The calculation underlying this and future redistributions
of voting power is based on size of economic output (50 percent),
openness (30 percent), variability (15 percent), and the size of foreign
reserves (5 percent). As a result of the adjustment, America yielded
0.29 percent of its IMF votes, to be left with 16.73 percent. The IMF,
as noted earlier, requires an 85 percent majority of its members to make
any important changes to the way it operates. Figures 4.1 to 4.3 show
the different levels of influence in the world according to economy and
IMF votes.

Figure 4.1   Influence by IMF Votes 2009

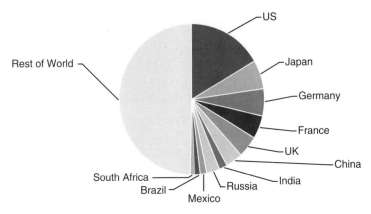

Source: IMF

Figure 4.2   Influence by Size of Economy 2008

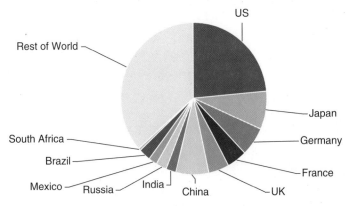

Source: IMF

The IMF commented on the voting reform as follows:

The approved quota and voice reform signals the beginning, rather than the end, of a process. It recognizes that country representation will need to adjust to changes in the global economy further down the road. Specifically, the agreement provides that realignments of quota and voting shares will take place every five years—which will result in a further increase in the share of under-represented countries.[7]

Figure 4.3   Influence by Size of Economy 2014 (est.)

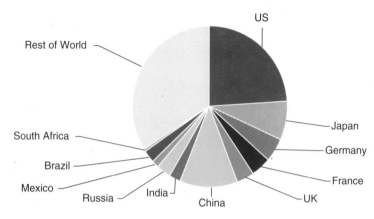

Source: IMF

Given the calculation on which voting power is based, it is inevitable that China, India, and other fast-growing emerging countries will increase their share of the IMF's votes, at the expense of the more developed, slower-growing countries, some of whom will have shrunk significantly in size by the end of 2010. The financial crisis and the shrinking of the American economy which resulted from the economic slowdown make it only a question of time before America's voting share in the IMF falls below the 15 percent required to maintain a blocking vote. Five months after the IMF approved the much discussed and hard-negotiated changes in voting power, in September 2008 the IMF Managing Director Dominique Strauss-Kahn established a Reform Committee to examine options for overhauling the IMF, with the following words:

Important progress has been made in the reform of the Fund's governance, including the initiation of a process to realign members' voting power within the Fund. However, the task of enhancing the Fund's legitimacy and effectiveness must also come to grips with the question of whether the significant changes since the establishment of the Fund require reform of the institutional framework through which members' voting power is actually exercised. Among other things, this requires careful

> *consideration of the respective roles and responsibilities of the Board of Governors, the International Monetary and Financial Committee, the Executive Board, and Fund Management.*[8]

The committee that was nominated to undertake this task at the IMF consisted of eight prominent academics and public sector finance officials, chaired by the widely respected Finance Minister of South Africa, Trevor Manuel, and with good developing country representation, although none from China. But by the time the committee's report was produced six months later, the name of Zhou Xiaochuan, the Governor of the Chinese central bank, the People's Bank of China, appeared as the ninth Committee member. China saw an opportunity to be involved at the grassroots in the IMF reform process, and was able to persuade the IMF to make a ninth seat available on the Reform Committee. The committee's report, which was produced on March 24, 2009, argues directly for fundamental changes in the IMF's governance. If these are carried out, they will place the IMF in advance of any other global organization in terms of the adjustment made to its structure and operation to reflect a much changed world. The report states in its preamble that "the world has changed dramatically since the Fund's founding, yet the key features of the Fund's governance structures have not."[9] It comments that "the changes in voting power approved in April 2008 were small, in comparison with the changes which had occurred globally, and the timetable for making them was painfully slow." It recommends that the next set of voting adjustments to the IMF be brought forward to early 2010. A new governance approach should be adopted, with each of the IMF's governing bodies undergoing significant change, and a council being appointed that is drawn from all 185 members of the IMF "since the governance of globalization requires a strong multilateral framework," meeting at least twice a year to oversee the IMF's work at the strategic level. The Managing Director of the IMF, who since 1945 has always been a European, should in future "be a world figure or symbol representing global financial stability," and "the selection of the Managing Director should occur through a transparent, open and merit-based system."

The committee's other recommendations focused on reducing the influence of America and the other larger shareholders (led by Japan, Germany, France, and Britain) and improving the effectiveness of the IMF's operations. China supports extensive reform of the IMF and the World Bank, the two key global multilateral institutions. This position was set out in a speech made to the boards of World Bank and IMF Governors at their annual meeting in October 2008 by a deputy governor of China's central bank, Yi Gang:

China attaches significant importance to the role of the Bretton Woods institutions . . . From the medium and long-term perspective, the Fund must address the inherent deficiencies of the current international monetary system and foster an international financial architecture adaptive to the evolving global economy and financial markets . . . the World Bank should urge the developed countries to shoulder their due responsibilities in stabilizing the global economy through targeted measures, carried out in an even-handed and professional fashion . . . Enhancing the voice and representation of developing and transition countries in the World Bank's decision-making process is an essential component of its governance . . . the ultimate achievement of a 50/50 distribution of its voting rights is the most fundamental and important of World Bank reforms.[10]

At the G20 summit in April 2009 in London, the world leaders present, who included representatives of all the major IMF members, made the IMF the central multilateral vehicle for meeting the economic crisis, with specific responsibility for cooperating with the Financial Stability Board to oversee all the G20 countries plus Spain and the European Union. Its resources were trebled to US$750 billion, its own finances were strengthened with a large subscription to its share capital, and its plan to sell some of its gold holdings to aid the poorest countries was supported. The summit recognized the IMF's steps towards reform, called for the next IMF voting realignment to be brought forward by two years to 2011, and scheduled the World Bank for the same reform treatment as the IMF by the spring of 2010.[11] The economic weakness of the Western developed countries will make it easier for these initiatives—which shift power away from the developed world—to be followed up. At the same time, China's role at the G20 London summit was not as assertive as many had expected. The summit host Gordon Brown, Prime Minister of the host country Britain, had talked previously about a very large package of financial support for the world economy. The Chinese delegates to the summit, representing the country with the largest pile of foreign reserves in the world, must have expected Brown to turn to them for a large contribution. But the most they were prepared to commit was US$40 billion, by way of a loan, to contribute to the IMF's US$500 billion of new funding which would support new lending to countries challenged by the harsh economic downturn. Japan's contribution, by way of contrast, was US$100 billion. An observer at the London summit commented as follows:

> *When the meeting ended, it was clear that China was not in a hurry to claim the mantle of leadership, but neither was it willing to play the traditional second fiddle. China has in fact acted in a fashion that will be immediately familiar to long time observers of the Middle Kingdom. It does not want to be perceived as an outlier to the international community, and even less to be isolated. But neither will it put itself on the line for major multilateral responsibilities.*[12]

China's guarded reticence at the London summit in April 2009 was surprising in view of the release a few days prior to the summit of a proposal posted on the Chinese central bank's Web site by the central bank governor Zhou Xiaochuan, which criticized the use of the US dollar as the world currency, and suggested that an alternative reserve currency could be created which is:

> *... disconnected from individual nations and is able to remain stable in the long run, thus removing the inherent deficiencies caused by using credit-based national currencies.*[13]

This currency proposal flew in the face of encouraging signs that China and the United States were getting closer together, following a courtship by a United States suddenly acutely aware of its dependence on China with the object of forming a configuration involving just two countries—China and the United States—in a grouping which has become known as G2. As separate chapters in this book examine China's possible interest in replacing the dollar as the world currency and the US–China relationship, suffice it to say here that although China considers its relationship with the United States to be strategically its most important bilateral relationship, it does not want to get drawn into a one-to-one relationship which might limit its options.

Indeed, it is generally believed that the Shanghai Cooperation Organization (SCO)—involving Russia, China, and the four central Asian states of Kazakhstan, Kyrgyzstan, Tajikistan, and Uzbekistan, with Iran, India, Pakistan, and Mongolia as permanent observers—was founded by Russia and China in 2001 as a counter to American influence in Central Asia, a region whose energy resources make it of strategic significance to global oil majors both Chinese and Western. This impression was confirmed in 2005 when the United States sought, and was denied, observer status to the Shanghai Group, and further emphasized by a series of declarations issued at the meetings which stated that the SCO leaders think that the stability and security of Central Asia can only be achieved through the efforts of the regional states. The SCO has effectively warned the United States not to get further involved in Central Asia, a region which Russia and China regard as their backyard. Although in March 2009 the United States was invited to send a representative, not even of observer status, to the SCO meeting in Moscow on Afghanistan, China and Russia will never allow the US to play any important role in the SCO.

The crisis has thrust China quickly onto the world stage, into a role which in some ways it is not prepared for. It is clear that in addition to protecting its own economic and sovereignty interests, China is pushing hard for fundamental reform of the large international financial institutions headed by the IMF and the World Bank, where it can see that it can exercise its influence. Within a few years the governance of these institutions will have changed dramatically, with a greater degree of involvement by the major emerging countries. This will dilute the influence and marginalize the involvement of the older European members, and will also greatly reduce the United States' influence by removing its blocking vote. The result will be to institutionalize the shift of power away from the US and Europe—a process that has been accelerated by the credit crisis—towards the emerging countries, particularly those in Asia. The G8 is too restrictive and exclusive a grouping to be able to accommodate this shift. Its role will be overtaken by the G20 and the two multilateral institutions that were designed by the architects of the Bretton Woods agreement over 60 years ago. The world is set for fundamental change in governance on a scale not seen since 1945. China may never be in a position to take over the kind of global leadership role played by the United States since 1945. But it will play a steadily larger role, often behind the scenes, and often via one of the multilateral organizations such as the IMF. China's influence will encourage the larger developing countries, including Turkey, Egypt and Saudi Arabia, Nigeria and South Africa, Turkey and Iran, Brazil and Mexico, as well as India to become much more prominent in global affairs over the next one or two decades. The hinge for these developments will be the relationship between the United States and China, the two most powerful countries in the world—a relationship which is covering an ever wider range of important issues, including the role of the dollar as the world currency.

Endnotes

1. Transcript of interview Wen Jiabao with Lionel Barber, editor of the *Financial Times*, February 2, 2009.
2. See letter from Ambassador Negroponte to President of the UN Security Council dated March 20, 2003.
3. Data and statistics, World Bank Web site http://www.worldbank.org.
4. Council on Foreign Relations http://www.cfr.org, November 15, 2008.
5. Ibid.
6. IMF Press Release 08/278 November 9, 2008.
7. IMF Press Release 08/93 April 2008.
8. IMF Press release 08/200 September 4, 2008.

9. Committee on Governance Reform, Final Report, IMF, March 24, 2009.
10. Statement by the Hon. Yi Gang, Governor of the Fund for the People's Republic of China, at the Joint Annual Discussion, October 13, 2008.
11. London Summit—Leaders' Statement, April 2, 2009.
12. Francis Godemot, *Yale Global*, April 24, 2009.
13. "Reform the International Monetary System," Zhou Xiaochuan, People's Bank of China Web site, March 24, 2009.

An End to Dollar Dominance?

No bigger symbol exists of America's place in the world than the widespread use of the US dollar in the world's financial capitals, in the pricing of oil, gold, and every other major commodity, and in international trade. Suggestions that the dollar's role as the world currency should cease strike at the heart of US global dominance. The dollar has been the payment standard for longer than almost everyone alive today can remember. Its supremacy as a medium of pricing, a store of value, and a means of payment for trade and finance is taken for granted. Although academics, currency experts, and central bankers from John Maynard Keynes onwards have recognized the problems inherent in using one country's currency as a world currency, the dollar has continued in its global role for over 60 years, because the perceived benefits to be gained from changing to a new, better, but untried system have not been large enough to outweigh the costs of continuing with a system that has worked most of the time. Needless to say, a change to a monetary system which did not have the dollar at its core would also have to overcome resistance from the United States, who benefits considerably from the dollar's world currency role.

The 2008 crisis originated in the American financial system. The financial instability that caused the crisis was partly the result of the dollar's role of world currency. This role was also important in quickly transmitting the effects of the crisis around the globe. The crisis has had such severe global consequences that central bankers and financial economists studying the causes of the crisis are revisiting the composition and operation of the world currency as an issue which may urgently need reform. China, which has attracted a new level of interest and respect from the financial community since the crisis by virtue of the size of its reserves and the growth potential of its economy, has used its new profile to highlight the dollar's world currency role as a fundamental cause of the crisis, and to call for change. Such is the level of support from Russia and other important developing countries for China's initiative that, for the first time since the dollar's role as the world currency was established at the Bretton Woods meeting in 1944, the replacement of the dollar as the world currency by a different system has moved from being an ideal with largely academic support to being a practical and possibly desirable alternative supported by a wide range of central bankers and finance ministers as well as academic experts.

As the world currency, the dollar must serve two masters. First and foremost, it is the currency of the United States of America. Its second role is to provide the world with a liquid means of payment for trade, a store of value, and a unit of account. Countries hold large quantities of dollars as their rainy-day reserves. The years leading up to the 2008 crisis were a time of rapid world growth, arising from globalization. As the world currency, the dollar was called on to provide most of the liquidity for this growth. The level of foreign reserves held in dollars by central banks around the world, mostly in developing countries, grew at an average annual rate of 18 percent during this time, greatly increasing the potential foreign claims on the dollar.[1] (Figure 5.1 shows world foreign exchange reserves held in US dollars from 2001 to 2008.)

Figure 5.1 World Foreign Exchange Reserves Held in US$

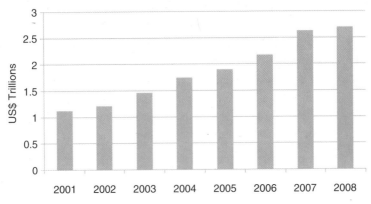

Source: IMF

This growth vastly increased dollar liquidity financed by dollar-denominated debt. The American credit crisis was the result of too much debt. The dollar's role as world reserve currency in a growing, globalized world which needed more reserves contributed to that debt excess.

A New Global Currency?

In March 2009, a week or two before the London Summit of the G20 to discuss measures for stabilization and reform of the world's financial system, two independent calls were made by respected institutions to replace the dollar as the world currency with some other monetary unit. One call was made in the preliminary report of the Commission of Experts established in December 2008 by the UN General Assembly to examine the financial crisis and suggest reforms.[2] The commission was chaired by Professor Joseph Stiglitz, a Nobel Prize winner and a former Chief Economist of the World Bank. The 17 other members of the commission included three central bank governors, several current or former ministers of finance, and various other acknowledged currency experts from around the world. On March 19, 2009, the commission produced its preliminary report, ahead of the meeting at the General Assembly held at the end of March to discuss reforms of the international financial system. The report began:

> *The rapid spread of financial crisis from a small number of developed countries to engulf the global economy provides tangible evidence that the international trade and financial system needs to be profoundly reformed to meet the needs and changed conditions of the 21st century.*

It called for the establishment of a new global reserve system, commenting that:

> *... the global imbalances which played an important role in this crisis can only be addressed if there is a better way of dealing with international economic risks facing countries than the current system of accumulating international reserves. To resolve this problem, a new Global Reserve System ... could contribute to global stability, economic strength and global equity. Currently, poor countries are lending to the rich countries at low interest rates. The dangers of a single-country reserve system have long been recognized, as the accumulation of debt undermines confidence and stability. But a two (or three) country reserve system, towards which the world seems to be moving, may be equally unstable. The new Global Reserve System is feasible, non-inflationary and could be easily implemented ...* [3]

Although the UN Expert Commission marks a watershed in the evolution of a world currency, its preliminary report did not attract much attention from world markets. But four days later, on March 23, 2009, the markets, more sensitive to developments in China than in the UN, did react to a paper that appeared on the Web site of the Chinese central bank, under the name of the governor Zhou Xiaochuan, entitled "Reform the International Monetary System." The paper started:

> *The outbreak of the current crisis and its spillover into the world confronts us with the long existing but still unanswered question: what kind of*

international reserve system do we need to secure global financial stability
and facilitate world economic growth, which was one of the purposes for
establishing the IMF?[4]

It questioned the dollar's role in the context of the new, more stable international financial system that the crisis had highlighted as essential, and argued for the dollar's replacement by another kind of currency unit. This new unit should not be the currency of one country, but should stand above all existing currencies as a supra-national currency. The paper was immediately picked up by the media. On March 24, London's financial newspaper, the *Financial Times*, commented:

China yesterday threw down a challenge to America's 50-year dominance of the global economy as it proposed replacing the dollar as the world's main reserve currency with a new global system under the control of the International Monetary Fund. In a muscle-flexing move that will be seen as an attempt to exploit the big shifts in economic power created by the recession sweeping the West, Beijing said that the dollar's role could eventually be taken over by the IMF's so-called Special Drawing Right (SDR), a quasi-currency that was created in 1969 . . . China's central bank governor has delivered a powerful message to the world this week. He wants an end to the dollar era. This is not sabre-rattling. He has made serious proposals for a reserve currency to rival the greenback and he deserves a hearing . . . Beijing now wants to play an active role in reshaping the world monetary order. This outward-looking view should be welcomed.[5]

When the American Treasury Secretary, Timothy Geithner, heard about the Chinese proposal the day after it appeared on the Chinese central bank's Web site, he said it "deserves some consideration."[6] Such was the level of uncertainty regarding the effect of the crisis on the American banking system, and such were the expectations of China's role in the forthcoming London summit, that the dollar immediately fell sharply against the euro and other major currencies as soon as news of Geithner's comment reached the foreign exchange markets.

Tim Geithner was forced to issue a same-day clarification, saying that the dollar would remain the world's dominant reserve currency for "some time to come," and that he had not read the proposal from the Chinese central bank governor.

Others, however, were of a different mind. Two days later, Andrey Denisov, the deputy Russian foreign minister, was reported by the Russian news agency as saying that Russia wanted to convene an international conference at ministerial level to discuss the creation of a new global currency. The report quoted Denisov as follows:

This proposal is aimed at a practical realization of the idea about a new global accounting unit or a new global currency. It is a question which should be discussed to create a consensus. One way or another, we will have to do it, if we are seriously talking about reforms.[7]

He said that, in the long term, global currency reform was inevitable, and that India, South Korea, Brazil, and South Africa supported the proposal, in addition to China and Russia. But at the subsequent G20 Summit in London, nothing was heard about any change in the role of the dollar. The Chinese, having thrown their stone into the pool, went quiet on the issue, preferring to allow some time to let the ripples from the stone spread and the idea to sink in. The genie had been let out of the bottle. Could it be put back?

The Chinese governor's paper, which was published online, concisely summarized a case—which had emerged over many years of academic thought and investigation—for examining the dollar's role and considering an alternative arrangement. His proposal linked the financial crisis with the use of the dollar as the world currency, by attributing the cause of the crisis to excessive amounts of credit created in the United States, the home of the dollar. Once debt began to overload the American financial system, he argued, the problem was bound to spread because of financial globalization and the close interrelationships between world security markets, which are linked directly by the dollar to the world's largest financial markets which are based in New York. He pointed out that a world currency needs to be anchored to something solid. Its issue should not be arbitrary, but governed by rules that are transparent. The currency needs to be flexible enough to respond to changes in economic activity. It should be disconnected from the individual circumstances of any one country, because these individual country circumstances will conflict with world needs for a currency which provides stability and a store of value. The Chinese proposal was based on a return to the original thoughts that inspired the creation of the IMF and the new world order in 1944, before it was decided to make the dollar the world currency. China's proposal referred back to the time at the end of the Second World War when the superpower status of the US was expressed not just in multilateral institutions such as the IMF and the World Bank, but also in the dominant role of the US currency, which reflected overwhelming US economic strength at that time. One of the biggest issues that had to be decided at Bretton Woods in 1944 was the choice of a currency unit for the new world economic order. The United States turned down Keynes' proposal for a currency which would be issued by the IMF and backed by a basket that included gold and 29 other commodities. Instead the Americans adopted their own variation on the gold standard, which linked all currencies to the dollar, itself convertible into gold at a fixed rate. The United States' choice of the dollar as the world currency in 1944 contravened Keynes' and others' view, that to use one country's currency as the world currency would create volatility in the world economy, once growth became strong enough to outpace the supply of currency. But the overriding strength in 1944 of the American economy, the credibility of its finances, and the weakness of any competitors were irresistible arguments in favor of the dollar at that time. Its world role became part of the Bretton Woods settlement in 1945.

The Chinese drew attention to the disadvantage of using a world currency which also serves as the currency of one country, because the different objectives of a national currency and the world currency cause global financial and economic instability. The power of the currency-issuing country to manage its own economy is weakened by the use around the world of its own currency in payment and as a store of value in monetary reserves. Every dollar held as an asset on an overseas central bank balance sheet is a liability of the American Government. The advantage of using a supra-national currency, rather than the dollar or another national currency, is that the issue of a non-national currency at times of strong global liquidity demand, when economic growth is strong, is not constrained by the excessive build up of liabilities in the country that issues the currency. Furthermore, with a supra-national currency, the changes reflected by prices of important commodities such as oil, copper, and timber are not changes in the value of the dollar but simply changes in underlying supply and demand. Greater commodity price stability would result from using a supra-national currency rather than the dollar, as volatility in the price of the dollar would no longer be reflected in the prices of oil and other important commodities.

The Special Drawing Right

The Chinese proposal summarized many of the problems inherent in using the dollar as a world currency. It went a step further and addressed the question of what should replace the dollar, resurrecting the original IMF suggestion that the Special Drawing Right or SDR (a unit of account later created by the IMF in 1969) could be used as a world currency for trade and reserve management. Made up of specified amounts of various country currencies, the SDR was created as a monetary unit additional to gold and the dollar, to provide global liquidity, to be managed outside the control of any one government by the IMF, itself answerable to virtually all the countries in the world. The SDR is presently composed of the four largest, fully convertible currencies used in world trade, in proportions which were last set in 2005 (and are revised every five years) as follows: US dollar 44 percent, Euro 34 percent, and the Japanese yen and pound sterling 11 percent each.[8] The Chinese proposal argued that the SDR could be a reliable store of value if it contained fixed amounts of each country's currency (not just the main four currencies), and if reserves were held at the IMF to back it. The IMF would be the issuer and guarantor of the SDR. Its use as the world currency would turn the IMF into a world central bank, with control over world interest and inflation rates, and hence with considerable economic and political power. This power would derive from its role as the issuer and guardian of the world currency, a role presently occupied by the United States. According to IMF data, at the end of 2008 the proportion of global currency reserves held in US dollars was 20 percent higher than the dollar weighting in the SDR, at 64 percent.[9] If the SDR became the world currency, the reweighting of international reserves to mirror the composition of the SDR would incline central banks to sell a large amount of dollars from their reserves, and add euros.

The use of the SDR as a world currency has been criticized by some commentators, including the famous American investor Jim Rogers, because the SDR cannot be a "real" currency.[10] But similar criticisms were made of the euro, a "real" currency, prior to its introduction as the European currency in 1999. The euro was a new currency made up of fixed amounts of the Deutschemark, the French franc, the Dutch guilder, and other existing European currencies, in the same way as the SDR is made up of existing major world currencies. Critical to the euro's success was: the creation of its own central bank, the European Central Bank, to conduct credible monetary policy within the area covered by the currency; the backing of the main European countries, France and Germany, together with their reserves; the eventual abandonment of national currencies; and agreements by the countries within the euro to contain national debt within set limits. The result is that the euro is now probably the world's most trusted currency. It turns out that an unswerving commitment to the euro by Germany and France, Europe's most important economic players, was sufficient to ensure the new currency's success, notwithstanding the participation of countries with a much less disciplined financial record, for example Italy and Greece.

The success of the euro demonstrates that all of these steps are possible in the case of the SDR, but, by the same token, the SDR could only succeed as a world currency if it enjoyed the full support of the world's major economic units. A commitment to the SDR by the United States, Europe, China, and Japan, who together account for 70 percent of world GDP in 2009, would be required to balance the participation in the unit of many other smaller countries with more uncertain and volatile economic prospects. National currencies existed alongside the euro for several years before the euro took over completely: it could be possible for major currencies to coexist beside the world currency for a long period. Like the euro, the SDR would have to have its own central bank or monetary authority, there would have to be some agreement on budget deficits between the main countries involved, and member countries would need to allocate foreign reserves to supporting the world currency. This kind of international cooperation appears to be unrealistic, until one considers the level of financial cooperation between countries that already has to occur, by default, in support of cross-border economic cooperation and currency alignment. The operation of a world currency would provide a framework within which this "de-facto" cooperation could occur systematically.

Using the enlarged SDR as the world currency, instead of the dollar, would have the great advantage of delinking the indebted American economy from its close relationship with the world economy. The use of the dollar as the world currency harnesses the peaks and troughs of the world economic cycle to the American economy, and vice versa. In 1945, this relationship was seen as necessary for hitching an impoverished and war-torn world to American economic muscle. But does the cost now outweigh the benefit? The view taken by the UN Expert Committee, supported by the most important emerging countries, is that it does. On June 15 and 16, 2009, the first summit to be held by the four so-called BRIC countries—Brazil, Russia, India, and China—issued a communiqué which expressed the need for a "diversified, stable and predictable currency system." After the summit, Russian officials strongly criticized the global financial architecture, saying the dominance of the US dollar risked instability in currency markets.[11]

China and the World Currency

Although the case made both by the UN Commission and by the Chinese central bank governor for a new reserve currency to replace the dollar appeared to be strong, suspicions arose as to China's motives for making a proposal at this time which could weaken American power. It is widely known that China has presently about 70 percent of its foreign reserves invested in American debt. In March 2009 Chinese Premier

Wen Jiabao took the opportunity presented by a widely televised press conference following the annual Party Congress in Beijing to voice a concern over the security of Chinese assets invested in the US. This direct message, from China to the United States via the world's press, is unusual. As such matters are normally left to the strategic dialogue between the two countries, such a public statement is an indication of the level of concern felt by the Chinese that the Fed's policy of money creation to ease the deep US recession could cause the international value of the dollar to depreciate. In turn, this would undermine the dollar's role as a store of value for foreign investors in American securities, of which China is the largest. China can limit the negative impact of higher American interest rates on the American debt it holds by keeping American bonds until they mature and are redeemed at their par value. But it cannot avoid large falls in the value of the American currency, which would reduce the value of its savings when its American investments are sold and converted back into its own currency, the yuan. The Chinese can see that their foreign reserves will continue to increase in the next few years, because it will take some time for the Chinese savings rate to fall significantly. Surpluses will continue to accrue on China's trading in tangible goods with other countries. Meanwhile, the dividends and interest which accrue every day on China's huge pile of foreign assets will heavily outweigh in size the interest payments which China has to make to foreigners who hold China's debt. China will need to find a home for these large capital accruals that at least preserves spending power in line with the increase in Chinese wages.

The rapid aging of China's population mentioned earlier is a vitally important factor in the management of China's pile of savings. Not only will China's working population not increase after 2010 and its over-60 population start to balloon, but in 2030, around the time when China is set to overtake the United States to become the world's largest economy, its overall population will start to shrink. With the estimated ratio of Chinese working adults to over-60 retirees set to worsen from 6 to 1 in 2005 to 4.4 to 1 in 2015 and 3.8 to 1 in 2020, the pressure on China's need to save will remain strong.[12] China has only a few years to build up its savings before it needs to start drawing them down to provide its people with a basic income in retirement, which most

Chinese presently lack. In the matter of investment returns, the sudden turnaround in China's demographic statistics, from favorable in the three decades to 2010 to increasingly unfavorable in the three decades to 2040, gives China much less room to maneuver than suggested by its large pile of foreign reserves, presently around US$2 trillion and rising. It underlines both China's need for a reliable store of long-term value in which it can invest, and its concerns about the possible long-term depreciation of the dollar as a way for the US to minimize its debt obligations in real terms.

The United States and the World Currency

The United States clearly derives economic benefit and influence from the use of the dollar as the world trading currency. American debt can be financed much more easily and cheaply in dollars than in another currency which carries additional risk deriving from the exchange rate fluctuation against the dollar. A large part of the profits made by the American central bank from issuing American currency would be lost if the dollar ceased to be the world currency. The dollar's world currency role allows American economic policy to influence the economic policies of other countries. Americans have grown up believing that the dollar's supremacy is a mark of American superiority. The loss of world currency status would be a blow to American pride, and the loss of benefits suffered by the United States from the end of the dollar's role as the world currency would be comparable to the loss of influence suffered by Britain when the Bretton Woods agreement in 1945 brought an end to the major world currency role for the pound. If the IMF, in place of the United States Treasury and Federal Reserve Board, were to become the issuer and guardian of the world currency, in line with the Chinese proposal, and if the American vote in the IMF was to be diluted in accordance with proposals for change presently under discussion, the United States could soon find itself voting in the IMF on nearly equal terms with China. One can imagine that the American Government will try to preserve the dollar's role as the global currency, and maintain the role of the

US Federal Reserve Board. But can a United States wounded and weakened by the financial and economic crisis resist efforts to undermine its global influence? While inertia is on its side, the US may not be able to prevent the eventual replacement of the dollar as the world currency. One reason is that the damage to the US financial system and economy has been very serious and will take years to repair, while economic growth in China and other important developing countries will probably recover quite quickly. Another is that the objective case for replacing the dollar as the world currency with another system is recognized by a number of countries as having merit.

An end to falling house prices is a minimum requirement for the US economy to start to stabilize. The American housing boom was so big, and the overshoot so great, that it may take four or five years from the high point reached in early 2007 before the American housing market is in a position to start moving up again. American banks also have a wave of defaults in credit card and other debt to deal with. An economic recession caused by inflationary overheating normally requires only one or two years for inflation to be brought down via higher interest rates, and then for the economy to be restarted via monetary easing and fiscal injections. But a debt-driven recession is a more fundamental problem, requiring years of retrenchment and deleveraging by households and companies. It took Asia seven years to recover from the Asian financial and economic crisis which started in 1997. So the United States, whose 2008 financial crisis was every bit as serious as the 1997 Asian crisis, will do well to have completed its deleveraging by 2010. In fact, it may take the US until 2012 or 2013, or longer, to adjust its debt, recover its economic poise, and start growing sustainably again. Moreover, the crisis has changed the structure of America's economy, particularly its banking system. The American Government has become the controlling shareholder in several key financial enterprises, including the world's largest insurance company AIG and one of the largest bank brokerages Citigroup. It will take years to disentangle itself from these necessary but unwanted and economically damaging commitments. The change in the structure of the American economy, with a much greater degree of government ownership and a smaller and much weaker financial sector, could lower the American medium-term annual economic growth rate from three or four percent to nearer two percent.

By 2013, both the Chinese and Indian economies will have been growing at between eight percent and 10 percent a year for at least two years. Other Asian economies, including Japan, will have switched more trade towards these two big economic growth engines, continuing the shift in the balance of the world economy towards Asia, and away from the United States and Europe. In 2012, according to projections based on purchasing power prepared by the IMF and publicized in its database, the share of the world economy occupied by China and India will be larger, at 19.6 percent, than America's share of world output at 19.1 percent. By 2014, China and India together will account for 21.2 percent of the world economy, and the US for 18.3 percent.[13] Although the actual out-turns will naturally differ from the projections, the general direction is clear. It means that just as the US is starting to recover from its deep downturn, it will be overtaken in size by the combined economies of India and China, the two largest emerging countries. The US bargaining position has been weakened by the need to sell very large amounts of debt—at least US$3 trillion worth—over the next five years, with cash-rich foreign investors, of which China is the largest, needing to buy up to half.

The Argument for a New World Currency

The case against the dollar, or any national currency, acting as a world currency was clearly identified many years ago. Keynes made it the centerpiece of his proposals for a new monetary order at Bretton Woods. The same argument was well summarized 16 years later in the testimony of economist Robert Triffin before the United States Congress in 1960. Although Triffin was referring to a system of fixed exchange rates backed by gold, the arguments that Triffin used still hold water. If the dollar acts as the world currency, he said, the world depends on a steady flow of dollars from the United States to finance world trade and foreign country reserve growth. This outward flow of dollars requires the United States to run large deficits in its accounts with other countries. If these American external account deficits become too large, other countries may lose confidence in the value of the dollar. But if the United States moves to reduce its external deficits in order to restore confidence in the value of the dollar, the dollar flow to the rest of the world will be reduced and world growth will be cut as a result. In November 1960 Triffin stated to Congress:

A fundamental reform of the international monetary system has long been overdue. Its necessity and urgency are further highlighted today by the imminent threat to the once mighty US dollar.[14]

He recommended adopting another kind of unit as the world currency, an approach that could provide the liquidity the world needed for growth and reserve creation which did not require the United States to run large deficits with other countries. His view was supported by the comment made by Secretary of the Treasury Henry Fowler:

Providing reserves and exchanges for the whole world is too much for one country and one currency to bear.[15]

In 1960, when Triffin was addressing Congress, the US dollar was convertible into gold, so that when the central banks of foreign countries sent their dollars to the United States, they received gold back in return. As growth continued, the United States began to run short of gold. The need for an additional supply of liquidity became evident. In 1969 the IMF created another reserve unit, the Special Drawing Right, to meet this demand. In 1971, President Richard Nixon announced that the American Treasury would no longer redeem dollars for gold, and from 1973 the dollar started to float freely against most major currencies, as it does now. The post-1971 free-float acts to an extent as a self-correcting mechanism against large American deficits. In theory it should reduce the need for countries to hold large reserves because their currency should adjust automatically to changes in valuation through the floating mechanism. But a floating dollar is volatile, conflicting with the important need for it to act as a store of value (see above the aging problem faced by China from 2010 and the need to invest Chinese reserves safely as a consequence). Major over- and under-valuations of the dollar occur regularly, often as a result of the conflict between economic conditions in America and in the rest of the world. For example, in the period 1983 to 1985 the dollar became so overvalued, as a result of the domestic tight-money policies being pursued in the US, that in 1985 the major countries met to agree on ways to force the dollar down from its overvalued level in the so-called Plaza Accord. The volatility of the dollar, including long periods of major over- and under-valuation, encourages many countries, particularly developing countries, to save in the form of large dollar reserves as a precautionary defense, when spending more and saving less would be more beneficial both to them and everyone else. Because people require that a store of value should be stable, a floating dollar probably does tend to depress world demand and reduce economic activity below what it would be if some other kind of supra-national reserve currency system was in place. Large global imbalances persist, which follow from the conflict between domestic American policy requirements and global needs. The floating exchange rate system has not eradicated the problems that Keynes identified in 1944 and Robert Triffin described to Congress in 1960. The case for a supra-national currency is as strong now as it was when Triffin testified to Congress nearly 50 years ago.

The fact that the credit crisis started in the US, the result of ultra-loose credit driven by an apparently infinite supply of dollars, has drawn attention to the inherent weaknesses in the current world monetary system and to the dollar's world currency role. But what is the likelihood of a change, given the strong inertia inherent in the current system, however imperfect, together with the considerable loss of American benefit from giving up a dollar-based world monetary system? In ordinary times, the answer might be that a change is very unlikely. But the credit crisis, and the economic crisis which followed it, are not ordinary times. An event which increases the unemployment rate in the US to over 10 percent, and much higher than 10 percent in more vulnerable economies, can create a consensus for change. Moreover, the pre–financial crash driver of economic growth, the American consumer, has hit a wall, and will spend the next five or 10 years rebuilding savings and avoiding debt. Without the American consumer, where will the demand come from to drive the world economy along? The economic recovery, when it comes, could be slow and weak for a long time. If it is, for the first time it may be possible to persuade important decision-makers in developed countries, including the United States, that the world monetary system is holding growth back, and should be changed.

The Asian Region

China's active involvement in the debate over a world currency has drawn much attention, because on its own it accounts for about one-third of world foreign reserves, and if Hong Kong were included, more than that. Since the 1997 Asian crisis, China has been involved in a local Asian monetary system which provides liquidity to the smaller Asian economies, and operates as a local supplement to the global system. Both China and Japan underwrite with their reserves the inter-Asian monetary self-help scheme known as the Chiang Mai Initiative that started after the 1997 Asian crisis. The Asian countries believe that the main cause of the 1997 crisis was the aggressive speculative activity of hedge funds based in New York. The Chiang Mai system was started after the crisis to show would-be speculators that they would not be able to attack small Asian economies successfully. Countries who are short of dollars use the system to borrow dollars from each other. The large increase since 2002 in the foreign reserve pools held by China, Japan, and South Korea has allowed this intra-Asian monetary cooperation to develop. A more formal permanent arrangement between Asian countries could follow. An Asian Monetary Fund was proposed in 1997 during the Asian crisis, but was turned down at that time by the US Treasury on the grounds that international financial arrangements between countries should be controlled by Washington. It is an interesting reflection on the relative positions today of China and the United States that the US Treasury is probably not now in a position to prevent an Asian Monetary Authority, if China, Japan, and other Asian countries decided to set one up. The ultimate financial decision-maker now in Asia is not the US but China, who has begun to dominate the region ahead even of Japan and India by virtue of its economic growth and cash reserves.

Ahead of the London G20 Summit, China made its own currency available on a short-term loan basis to Asian neighbors who might suffer liquidity problems as a result of the crisis, a step interpreted as a conscious effort by China to develop the use of the Chinese yuan both within and beyond Asia as a more liquid, more local, and cheaper alternative to the dollar. In March, RMB 650 billion (US$95 billion) worth of currency swaps were established with Indonesia, Belarus, Malaysia, Argentina, Hong Kong, and South Korea. The *Financial Times* of London commented that these loans "indicate a more confident diplomacy and a larger future role in international finance for the Chinese currency."[16] These steps, to internationalize the yuan, are continuing.

The widespread use of the yuan as an Asian currency for trade and the pricing of commodities would be a big step in the exchange of Chinese for American monetary sovereignty in the region. By highlighting the demise of the dollar in an important region, it would strengthen further the case for a new kind of world currency. But it is unrealistic to expect the Chinese yuan to play the role of world currency. Not only would replacing the dollar with the yuan simply transfer the problems inherent in the existing system to a new one, and undermine the case for a supra-national currency, but China's financial system is years, probably many years, away from being able to operate openly and transparently. Its currency is still strictly controlled and unusable as the principal international means of investment and exchange. The yuan could not replace the dollar as the principal global means of exchange for the foreseeable future. Moreover, it is unlikely that the Chinese Government would want it to. Until China is able to generate strong new sources of domestic demand, the country's foreign trade will remain a vital source of growth, employment, and government tax revenue. Because Japan and other export-dependent Asian economies limit their own currencies' strength against the dollar, China believes that controlling the level of the yuan against the dollar provides China's exporters with a stable competitive position. This control would become impossible to maintain if the yuan started to be used widely around the world for financial transactions. Using the yuan as a world currency would also undermine China's case for replacing the dollar. However, the yuan could make up an important part of a new world currency, along with the dollar, other major currencies, and possibly a commodity basket.

China is preparing to share power with the United States. Nowhere is this truer than in the financial sphere, in which American global supremacy has suddenly dwindled, leaving regional powers to exercise greater financial influence. Although China's internal financial markets remain overcontrolled and underdeveloped, the country's economy is almost as large as Japan's, it is growing much faster, and the size of its reserves mean that China is already playing a more important global financial role than Japan. China cannot on its own bring an end to the dollar's global supremacy. But if it adds its considerable weight to a growing consensus, it can affect the outcome. The evidence from China's interventions in early 2009 shows that it prefers a supra-national currency to the dollar as a store of value, and it wants to bring that change about. The new currency unit may be the Special Drawing Right, made up of a basket of a wide range of currencies, reweighted every few months to reflect the relative shares in world output, and administered by the IMF. Or it may be something else. Arkady Dvorkovich, chief aide to the Russian Prime Minister Dmitry Medvedev, proposed at the BRIC summit in Yekaterinburg in June 2009 that the IMF SDR basket should be expanded to include the Chinese yuan, the currencies of commodity producers such as Australia and Canada, and possibly gold.[17] Whatever it is, such a move is receiving significant support from a wide range of experts, countries, and international bodies, including the UN.

When could the first moves to replace the dollar as the world currency occur? The timing will probably depend to a large extent on the speed with which the world emerges from its slowdown. If the recovery is slow and L-shaped, not fast and V-shaped, it is quite possible that a move to replace the dollar as the world currency could gather pace within the next year or two. The comments made at the BRIC press conference in June 2009 made it clear that the leading emerging countries were already considering ways of doing without the dollar. Although China's President was silent on the subject of currency reform, Dmitry Medvedev, Russia's president, said:

> *We have to consolidate the international monetary system, not only through the consolidation of the dollar but the creation of new reserve currencies.*[18]

Changes may take place faster than many presently consider possible. The consequence of this may well be that in 10 years, or even fewer, the latest announcement on interest rates from the US Federal Reserve Board will not move currency, commodity, bond, or stock prices like it does today. The focus of the markets will shift more to the real economy — growth, jobs, profits — because the level of the dollar, today a major source of uncertainty and market volatility, won't matter nearly so much. The relationship between China and the United States will play a critical role in this, as in many other global issues. We now turn to consider this relationship in more detail.

Endnotes

1. Data from Bloomberg.
2. Recommendations by the Committee of Experts of the President of the General Assembly on reforms of the international monetary and financial system, 63rd session, agenda item 48, March 19, 2009.
3. Ibid.
4. "Reform the International Monetary System," paper by Zhou Xiaochuan, published on People's Bank of China Web site, March 22, 2009.
5. "China Calls for New Reserve Currency," Jamil Anderlini, *Financial Times*, March 23, 2009.
6. "Geithner Affirms Dollar After Remarks Send It Tumbling," Anahad O'Connor, *New York Times*, March 25, 2009.
7. "Russia Adds to Calls for Currency Reform," Peter Garnham and agencies, *Financial Times*, March 26, 2009.
8. IMF Data http://www.imf.org.
9. Ibid.
10. CNBC interview, June 10, 2009.
11. "Emerging Powers Want Fair Global Economic Order," Isabel Gorst, *Financial Times*, June 17, 2009.

12. "China's Long March to Retirement Reform," Richard Jackson et al., Center for Strategic and International Studies, 2008.
13. IMF Data. http://www.imf.org.
14. System in Crisis 1959–1971, IMF op. cit.
15. IMF Data. http://www.imf.org.
16. "China and Argentina in Currency Swap," Jude Webber, *Financial Times*, March 31, 2009.
17. "Emerging Powers Want Fair Global Economic Order," Isabel Gorst, *Financial Times*, June 17, 2009.
18. Ibid.

6

Rowing the Same Boat: Sino–American Relations

On June 1, 2009, Treasury Secretary Tim Geithner found himself in Beijing speaking to a mostly Chinese audience at Peking University. Although the main purpose of his meetings was the same as his predecessor Henry Paulson, namely the development of economic and financial cooperation between China and America, his tone was very different:

China, despite your own manifest challenges as a developing country, you are in an enviably strong position . . . Business and households in the United States, as in many countries, are still experiencing the most challenging economic and financial pressures in decades . . . The extent of the damage to financial systems entails significant risk that the supply of credit will be constrained for some time. The constraints on banks in many major economies will make it hard for them to compensate fully for the damage done to the basic machinery of the securitization markets, including the loss of confidence in credit ratings. After a long period where financial institutions took on too much risk, we still face the possibility that banks and investors may take too little risk, even as the underlying economic conditions start to improve.[1]

Geithner's speech left no doubt that cooperation between America and China was at the center of his strategy for economic recovery:

China and the United States individually, and together, are so important in the global economy and financial system that what we do has a direct impact on the stability and strength of the international economic system. Other nations have a legitimate interest in our policies and the ways in which we work together, and we each have an obligation to ensure that our policies and actions promote the health and stability of the global economy and financial system.[2]

The crisis of 2008 shifted the economic and financial balance of power away from the United States and towards China. The leader of the world economic system, America, was compelled by its new circumstances to reach out to China as an equal partner, placing China in a position where it could set its own agenda.

Now that the credit crisis has made China indispensable to American and world economic growth, while China's expansion everywhere has brought it up against America's traditional global dominance, the future issue facing the world is how these two interdependent superpowers can overcome their turbulent past and work together. America needs to forge a policy of close cooperation with a country that historically has been more an enemy than a friend. In fact, for at least the first 30 years after the People's Republic founding in 1949, China and America were ideological opponents, who fought against each other in Korea and Vietnam, and who on several occasions nearly came to blows over Taiwan. For many years, the default setting for Sino–American relations was mistrust and misunderstanding, not friendly cooperation. Only a decade ago in the late summer of 1999, the front-running American presidential candidate George W Bush criticized President Bill Clinton's policy of constructive engagement with Beijing:

The president has made a mistake of calling China a strategic partner.
The next president needs to understand that China needs to be viewed
as a strategic competitor.[3]

But in an article published in January 2009 in the leading American
journal *Foreign Affairs*, investment banker and former US deputy Treasury Secretary Roger Altman wrote prophetically of the recent financial
crash:

... a few states, most notably China, will achieve a stronger relative
global position ... this crisis may lead to a closer relationship between the
United States and China. Trade-related flashpoints are diminishing,
which may soften protectionist sentiment in the US Congress. And
it is likely that, with Washington less distracted by the war in Iraq,
the new administration of Barack Obama will see more clearly than
its predecessor that the US–China relationship is becoming the United
States' most important bilateral relationship.[4]

A month or so later, in February, the fundamental importance of the
China relationship in American eyes was made clear by new Secretary
of State Hillary Clinton in a speech to the Asia Society in New York,
given a few days before her first foreign trip as Secretary of State:

... you know very well how important China is and how essential it
is that we have a positive, co-operative relationship. It is vital to peace
and prosperity, not only in the Asia-Pacific region, but worldwide.
Our mutual economic engagement with China was evident during the
economic growth of the past two decades. It is even clearer now in
economic hard times and in the array of global challenges we face, from
nuclear security to climate change to pandemic disease and so much else.[5]

The first meeting between China's President Hu Jintao and Barack
Obama, which took place at the G20 summit in London in April
2009, and which established a new strategic dialogue between the two

superpowers, was a huge contrast with the early days of President Obama's predecessor, George W Bush, who approved early in his first presidential term a larger-than-expected package of weapons to sell to Taiwan, emphasizing meanwhile America's readiness to come to Taiwan's defense should the island be attacked by China. America clearly needs China now much more than it did before, but does China need America as much? Is the new warmth in the Sino–American relationship sustainable? How did Taiwan, a small island off the Chinese coast, come to play such an important role in the relationship, and does it still matter?

History of the Relationship

Pearl Buck's best-selling novel *The Good Earth*, which won the Pulitzer novel prize in 1932 and later the Nobel Literature Prize, brought China to the awareness of the American public. But China was at war with itself, and Americans had to decide which of the warring Chinese factions to make friends with. In the propaganda struggle between the Chinese nationalists and the communists for the hearts and minds of the American people, first blood went to General Chiang Kai-Shek, leader of the Chinese nationalists, whose wife Soong Mei-Ling had been educated in America. Soong visited America frequently to preach the nationalist cause to large groups of American well-wishers. In 1937, she and her husband were featured on the cover of *Time* magazine as The Couple of the Year (Deng Xiaoping is the only other Chinese to have appeared as *Time*'s Person of the Year). But in 1938, Americans heard about a different kind of Chinese struggle, with the publication of Edgar Snow's book *Red Star Over China* in London and then in New York. Snow, an American journalist based in Beijing, was already engaged in writing a book about the Chinese communist movement when he managed to contact Mao and received an invitation to visit the communists at their hideout at Yan'an in northwest China for three months late in 1936. His popular book was based on his three-month stay with Mao. It brought the birth and early development of the Chinese communist party to an American audience, together with a detailed description of its leader Mao, who many outsiders believed had died on the Long March.

With Japan's military success in East Asia, which led to the defeat of Allied troops in Burma in 1942, China became important to the American war effort as a means of containing Japanese troops who were occupying half of China. The decisive factor in swinging American support behind the nationalists, and against the communists, was General Chiang's wife. Soong Mei-Ling was in a strong position to influence American minds. Her younger sister was married to Sun Yat-Sen, the doctor who inspired the Chinese Revolution in 1911, and her elder sister to the banker H H Kung, one-time Chinese Minister of Finance and rumored to be China's richest man between the wars. Most important of all, Soong Mei-Ling had graduated in 1917 as a Durant Scholar from first-rank women's college Wellesley, located near Harvard and the Massachusetts Institute of Technology. She toured America on behalf of her husband's nationalist cause, giving lectures to large groups of American citizens about the situation in China, even in 1943 addressing both houses of the United States Congress, the first woman to do so. *Life* magazine's report on her speech started:

Mme. Chiang's three hours at the Washington Capitol on February 19th are inevitably a part of US history. What she said and did there was up to the level of world events. Not only were Congressmen completely captivated by her but also hard-boiled reporters confessed they had never seen anything like it.[6]

As a direct result of her efforts, America contributed billions of dollars and large quantities of war material to supporting the Nationalist Chinese against the Japanese, starting even before Japan attacked Pearl Harbor in 1941. America's support for Taiwan since then has been due in significant part to its admiration for this charismatic, determined, and patriotic lady, who died in 2003 on Long Island, New York at the age of 106.

Soong Mei-Ling's efforts to win over American support for the nationalist cause and American anti-communism have been the most important long-term factors so far in Sino–American relations. When the Chinese nationalists were forced off the Chinese mainland by the communists to Taiwan, a small island off its southeastern coast, American support followed them. The American Government recognized the sovereign rights of Chiang Kai-Shek's government in Taiwan over the Chinese mainland, and after the Korean War started, sent the Seventh Fleet into the Taiwan Straits to signal to Beijing that America would stand behind the nationalists in Taiwan. Chiang Kai-Shek's nationalists in Taiwan became an outpost of American resistance in the Pacific to communist China which, allied with Russia, appeared to present a strong threat to the American presence in the Pacific. The experience of the Korean War, in which the Chinese drove back the Americans and their allies from the Chinese border by sheer weight of numbers, and the anti-communist witch-hunts inspired by Senator Joe McCarthy cast communist China as an enemy of America. The *Manchurian Candidate*, Richard Condon's 1959 novel portraying American soldiers captured and brainwashed by the Chinese during the Korean War to bring down the American Government, became a successful film released at the time of the Cuban missile crisis which encapsulated the American anti-communist paranoia of the time, and created dark images of evil Chinese communists which still populate the American imagination. On the three occasions when China threatened Taiwan in 1955, 1958, and 40 years later in 1995, America stood on each occasion between communist China and the recapture of Taiwan, providing vital military support to the Taiwanese and sending American battleships into the Taiwan Straits. In fact, both in 1955 and 1958 President Eisenhower's generals were surprised when he refused to allow the use of nuclear weapons on China's mainland to support Taiwan.

Against the strength of the tide running in Taiwan's favor, the start of an American relationship with Taiwan's enemy in Beijing came as a big surprise. Mao's split with the Soviet Union in 1960 increasingly threatened China along its very long Russian land border. In the late 1960s Mao started to think the unthinkable: a Sino–American alliance which would threaten the Soviets from two sides. After contact had been made with the United States by Chinese Embassy representatives, in 1971 Henry Kissinger secretly flew from Pakistan to Beijing to sound out the Chinese. The one-week visit of President Nixon to China in

1972 that followed—in response to an invitation from Mao—was a spectacular initiative that resulted in a marriage of convenience between two ideologically opposed powers looking for a counterweight to the Soviet Union. It achieved its main purpose, and was the prelude to America's recognition of Beijing seven years later.

But in the 1980s and 1990s, China started to change. The United States started to appear to Chinese eyes much more like the Promised Land than China's enemy. As China took up capitalism, the Chinese began to admire America's success and size. Go for growth; maintain stability; and do deals with America.[7] Reputedly, these were Deng Xiaoping's final instructions to Jiang Zemin, his successor as China's president in 1994. Although Deng, a Long March survivor, had been associated since adolescence with the struggles and triumphs of the Chinese Communist Party, by the end of his life he had realized that China's way forward lay down another road. He saw that economic growth and liberalization was China's future, that America and China would be the world's two economic giants for the next century or more, and that the world was not big enough for a China at loggerheads with the United States. China needed American help to be able to develop to the point where it could reach its potential. The ultimate pragmatist, he was ready to develop a serious long-term American relationship.

But it took the United States much longer to feel the same way about China. Although in January 1979 the United States transferred its diplomatic recognition from Taiwan's capital Taipei to Beijing, the *Taiwan Relations Act of 1979*, which guaranteed continued American support for Taiwan in the event of a Chinese invasion, showed that, even if the American head had crossed the Taiwan Straits to the mainland, the American heart was still in Taiwan. Over the next two decades it was not Beijing but Taiwan, and for a time the Soviet Union, that played the central role in Sino–American relations, as China's main significance for America continued to be as a counter to its northern neighbor. Continued American support for Taiwan through the 1980s and 1990s meant that even after the Soviet threat had disintegrated, American relations with China remained difficult. For instance, in 1995 President Lee Teng-hui of Taiwan accepted an invitation to visit his old American college Cornell which was approved by the US State Department. This recognition of Taiwan directly threatened China's policy of outlawing Taiwan internationally. It reacted by firing missiles and using military exercises to threaten Taiwanese voters ahead of the 1996 Taiwanese presidential election in which Lee Teng-hui was standing. President Clinton sent two carrier battle groups to the area, China backed off, and President Lee Teng-hui was re-elected.

The Effect of Terrorism on Sino–American Relations

With post-war American ally Japan the dominant economic power in East Asia, China simply did not carry enough weight in the 1990s to justify the United States relinquishing its support of Taiwan and Japan. America's relationship with Taiwan continued to stand in the way of the development of a strong, mutually trusting Sino–American relationship. But suddenly in the autumn of 2001, America needed a much better relationship with China. The terrorist attacks of 9/11 were a watershed in Sino–American relations. Before the attacks, American policy saw international threats as coming from rising major powers, with China as the most important future threat. But the success of al Qaeda's attacks on American soil turned the defeat of Islamic terrorism into the top American foreign policy objective. The attacks transformed China in America's eyes "from a strategic competitor requiring immediate attention, to a potential partner in the war on terror."[8]

NATO's deliberate bombing of the Chinese consulate in Belgrade on May 7, 1999 (referred to in Chapter 1) would certainly not have been approved by America after 9/11, because after September 2001 China's strategic importance to America was too great. Doubtless, China's downing of an American spy plane on Hainan Island in May 2001 as a retaliation to the consulate bombing would also not have happened if 9/11 had occurred a year earlier.

America's 9/11 also reshaped the Chinese view of the terrorist threat and heightened its importance. Since 1990, an organization calling itself the East Turkistan Islamic Movement—supported by the large non-Han Uygur population of the Western Chinese province of

Xinjiang, apparently working in collaboration with al Qaeda—actively pursued a terrorist strategy against Chinese forces, with the objective of creating an Islamic state allied with other Islamic movements to the west. After 9/11, China felt able to discuss its terrorist problem more openly with America and other potential allies. In October 2001, a meeting between Presidents Jiang Zemin and George W Bush on the fringes of the Asia Pacific Economic Cooperation Summit in Shanghai created a basis for a closer Sino–American dialogue on counterterrorism.[9]

The emergence of the North Korean nuclear program in 2002 also provided an important source of communication and cooperation between America and China. Both countries shared important common ground on North Korea. China did not see nuclear attack on its own soil by its ally North Korea as a possibility, but while wishing to prevent a regime collapse which would flood China with starving Korean refugees, did want to contain the spread of nuclear warheads from North Korea that might find their way into the hands of anti-Chinese terrorists based in Western China and elsewhere. The United States was similarly opposed to nuclear proliferation, and wanted to prevent any destabilization of East Asia. From the early part of the George W Bush presidency, America's fear of nuclear proliferation from North Korea gave China an ace that it could use with the Americans, as trade relations started to dominate the Sino–American relationship.

Playing off China's interest in Taiwan against the US strategic interest in North Korea and strengthening counterterrorist cooperation were the vital factors that kept Sino–American relations balanced, at a time when the violent American reaction to China's post-WTO explosion of exports to the United States would otherwise have seriously damaged the Chinese economy and completely disrupted the relationship. Without 9/11 it is possible, indeed likely, that American opposition to Chinese export penetration would have resulted in strong protectionist American measures being taken against China. As it was, the need of the American Government for Chinese cooperation in the anti-terrorist battle persuaded the George W Bush administration to prevent the introduction of laws in the American Senate from 2003 aimed at using higher import tariffs or a revalued Chinese currency to protect American products and workers from Chinese products.

America and China's Export Boom

China's formal entry into the World Trade Organization in 2001 opened the floodgates of China's export economy (see Figure 6.1), and Chinese products simply poured into Western markets. Ironically, American support was critical in getting China to join the WTO. President Clinton used the opening of a huge China market to American exporters and investors to obtain the general support of both Houses of Congress in 1999 for China's entry into the WTO. In a speech in early 2000 in Washington DC about China's entry to WTO, he commented:

> *Economically, this agreement is the equivalent of a one-way street. It requires China to open its markets, with a fifth of the world's population—potentially, the biggest markets in the world—to both our products and services in unprecedented new ways. All we do is to agree to maintain the present access which China enjoys. Chinese tariffs, from telecommunications products to automobiles to agriculture, will fall by half or more over just five years. For the first time, our companies will be able to sell and distribute products in China made by workers here in America, without being forced to relocate manufacturing to China, sell through the Chinese government or transfer valuable technology—for the first time. We'll be able to export products without exporting jobs.*[10]

As we now know, President Clinton was completely wrong, at least in the medium run. It was America, not China, that turned out to be the big potential market. Including Chinese exports shipped through Hong Kong as well as Chinese ports (as measured by American customs), Chinese exports to America rose over four times in nine years, from US$82 billion in 1999 to US$338 billion in 2008, an increase of US$256 billion. Over the same period, American exports to China increased by a relatively meager US$58.4 billion. The great trade expansion occurred between 2001 and 2005, when Chinese exports to America increased by 138 percent—at just the time when America most needed China's support for its invasions of Afghanistan and Iraq, and its so-called "war on terror." Between 1999 and 2008, China's overall

Figure 6.1   Share Taken of Chinese Exports by United States 2000–08

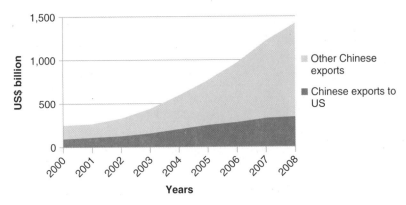

Source: US–China Business Council

surplus on its global trade was US$1 trillion, while its trade surplus with America was US$1.6 trillion.[11]

China's trading with America was absolutely critical to building up China's export industry and foreign reserves, developing the Chinese economy, and maintaining Chinese employment. Protecting the trade with America was the most important job that Chinese diplomats had in the early part of the decade which started in 2000. They were able to use American nerves over North Korea, al Qaeda, and the invasions of Afghanistan and Iraq as leverage for their diplomacy.

But even before 9/11 transformed America's strategic view of China, the impact of Chinese factories and Chinese output on the American labor market was starting to raise China's importance in Washington DC. As early as July 2001, the House Banking Committee of Congress held a hearing to discover the reasons for America's growing trade deficits. Former Federal Reserve Chairman Paul Volcker, former US Treasury Secretary Robert Rubin, and the chief economists of Morgan Stanley and Goldman Sachs testified as expert witnesses before American Senators, led by Charles Schumer from New York and former Goldman Sachs banker Jon Corzine from New Jersey. The findings were that America's increasing deficits were the result of America not saving enough. At this stage, blame for the deficits was not pinned on China and Japan, the major exporters to America. Robert Rubin's testimony emphasized the importance of maintaining free trade and preempted punitive tariffs against China and Japan, the two largest surplus countries:

> *Imports lower prices to consumers and producers, dampen inflation, and thereby lower interest rates, provide a critical role in allocating our resources to the areas where our comparative advantage is greatest, and, maybe most importantly, imports create competitive pressure for productivity improvement. All this is contributing greatly to our low levels of unemployment and to rising incomes at all levels that we have had in recent years . . . Increasing savings over the full business cycle would reduce imports and reduce the inflow of capital and, in my judgment, would be the most constructive approach to reducing the current account deficit . . .*[12]

Another witness called by the panel, Stephen Roach, chief economist of Morgan Stanley, started his testimony by stressing the shortage of American savings and the excess of American spending:

> *I believe that this imbalance should really be taken as a sign of a nation that has gone to excess, a US economy that in many important respects has lived beyond its means. America, as both Chairman Volcker and Treasury Secretary Rubin indicated, is a savings-short nation that has a voracious appetite to spend or consume.*[13]

The 2001 hearing was firmly agreed that the underlying cause of America's increasing trade deficits was the low American savings rate, which would have to rise. Increasing American trade deficits were not sustainable and would be corrected at some point by the market; exactly how was not known. Several participants noted the possibility of a violent reaction to excessive imbalances, at some unknown point.

But while the expert witnesses in Washington were blaming poor American savings habits for China's growing trade surpluses, concerns were growing elsewhere that Chinese exports were taking American jobs, and something should be done. In September 2001 an article appeared on CNN's online career page entitled "Could Your Job go to China?" It said in part:

> *Just as Friday's new Labor Department report shows the United States unemployment rate soaring in August to 4.9 percent from 4.6 percent, a newly released, federally funded study reveals that a significant number of production jobs are shifting from the American workplace to China ... What concerns Stephanie Luce, Ph.D., about her research data is not just her figure of at least 34,900 jobs—and maybe twice that—moving from the States to China in a seven-month period as a result of warming Washington–Beijing trade relations ... "What makes it worse," she says, "is that some of these are higher-wage jobs, the type of jobs that US cities have been fighting to win. And now they're leaving" ... The team discovered that more than 80 United States–based corporations had announced their intentions to shift production to China between October 1, 2000, and April 30 of [2001].*[14]

As public concerns over America's trade deficits with China grew, the government was coming under pressure to do something about them, and quick. But by now official American Government policy had shifted towards embracing China as a key ally in the fight against global terrorism. So in October 2003 American Treasury Secretary John Snow downplayed trade deficit concerns as best he could, arguing that he had discussed greater exchange rate flexibility with the Chinese as a way of addressing their increasing surpluses. He quoted the Chinese central bank governor as saying:

> *With the role of the market becoming increasingly important, the exchange rate of the RMB will be finally determined decisively by the market forces and have great flexibility.*[15]

Although in fact China's moves towards floating the Chinese currency were pedestrian, the American Government did its best to see the Chinese point of view, and managed American public opinion accordingly.

By 2005, the pressure on China and the American Government to correct the now huge Chinese surpluses had become intense. Senators from two American States which were affected by the ending of tariffs on imports of textiles at the end of 2004, Charles Schumer from New York and Lindsey Graham from South Carolina, brought a bill in February 2005 calling for the introduction of an import tax on Chinese goods of 27.5 percent. Schumer had been the chairman of the House Banking Committee four years earlier when the 2001 hearing on the balance of payments deficit (noted earlier) had concluded that the Chinese were not to blame. But politics is not economics, and Schumer, responding to the pressures being brought on him by his constituents in New York to limit Chinese competition, had become one of the most vocal advocates of anti-Chinese trade measures. The American Government used his bill as a lever to force the Chinese leadership to revalue the Chinese currency. By July 2005, something was done. The Chinese Government announced that the value of the yuan would be determined by supply and demand from China's main trading partners, and would be allowed to fluctuate up and down within daily limits. In practice this meant that the Chinese central bank managed the value of the Chinese currency, allowing it to float slowly upwards against the dollar. Within the first few days of the announcement, the yuan had appreciated by over 2 percent against the dollar, and the US Treasury Secretary was able to announce that the Chinese had already taken steps to correct the undervaluation of the Chinese currency. "We can tell you that we are not satisfied with simply a 2 percent revaluation," was Senator Schumer's response.[16] But after July 2005, Hank Paulson, who succeeded John Snow as US Treasury Secretary, was a powerful apologist for China. In his previous role as head of the large American investment bank Goldman Sachs, he had established in 2004 a joint venture in China with an office in Beijing, and had traveled many times to China. He made his views on China clear in a speech made in the Treasury in September 2006:

The prosperity of the United States and China is tied together in the global economy, and how we work together on a host of bilateral and multilateral issues will have a significant impact on the health of the global economy . . . Our prosperity is linked to the strength of foreign economies. And we are adversely affected by their economic declines and financial shocks . . . China has an increasingly important role in today's global economy and its economic relationship with the United States . . .[17]

Paulson argued that China was already a leading economy. Its demand was the primary factor in determining the price of commodities, such as oil, which were in the middle of a strong run up in price. He supported China, but called on it to take its own steps towards meeting its responsibilities as a leader. Paulson's direct contacts with the Chinese Government brought about a new era of close cooperation between America and China, and a longer term view of the relationship. His belief that close engagement with China was the best way to bring change produced a series of strategic dialogues that took place alternately in Beijing and Washington, which did more to raise common understanding than anything that had gone before. As the debate over China's trade surpluses turned from imposing tariffs to the need for a big Chinese currency revaluation, Paulson's seniority and relationship with China were extremely important in keeping America from attempting to force China to revalue its exchange rate.

But at a Senate Finance Committee hearing held in March 2006, entitled "US–China Economic Relations Revisited", Fred Bergsten, a widely respected economist attached to the Peterson Institute for International Economics, testified that China's currency was significantly undervalued, and that the trade imbalances which resulted were unsustainable. Gone was the argument championed five years earlier in the Senate hearing in 2001 by Robert Rubin of Citigroup and Stephen Roach of Morgan Stanley that correcting the imbalance between China and America depended on America saving more and spending less. Instead, Bergsten suggested an adjustment in the yuan–dollar rate of 20 to 40 percent, with an immediate revaluation of the Chinese currency of 10 percent and the rest to follow fairly quickly. Bergsten suggested that Paulson's strategy of constructive engagement with the Chinese should give way to a more proactive American policy:

It is obvious that China is extremely reluctant to make the needed changes in its currency policy. It is equally obvious that US efforts on the issue over the past three years, whether the earlier "quiet diplomacy" approach or the commendably more aggressive stance of the past six months or so, have borne little fruit.[18]

He suggested harsh measures should be taken by the United States. In a paragraph entitled "A US Strategy for China's Currency," he suggested various measures to force China to conform: labeling China as a currency manipulator as provided for under American law, preventing China from taking its place at the IMF, voting down the increase of China's IMF quota using the US blocking vote, and, as a last resort, imposing large tariffs on imported Chinese goods. As a bill to impose tariffs had already been framed by Senators Charles Schumer and Lindsey Graham, and another bill was waiting in the wings which described China as a currency manipulator, it would not have taken much time for Congress to put the necessary legislation into action.

Prior to the financial crash in 2008, the United States ran the largest trading deficits in its history, amounting to 7 percent of its GDP—twice the previous record of the 1980s. Such was the support within both Houses and in the country for action against China that it was only the pro-China stance of the Bush administration that stood between Congress and strong legislation aimed at Chinese imports. The impact on Sino–American relations of anti-China legislation would have been negative and lasting, making the cooperation entered into by both countries since the financial crisis much more difficult. It suited the American Government to exchange China's export penetration of the American market for China's assistance in fighting the terrorist threat, containing North Korea, and for allowing America a free hand in Central Asia. It was only Henry Paulson at the Treasury and George W Bush at the White House who stood between the US Congress and protectionism which would have led to a significant disruption of the Sino–American relationship. In the absence of efforts to increase the US rate of saving, for example through higher interest rates, the cost was a huge expansion of America's current account deficit and China's surplus, and an increasingly unbalanced global economy.

Effect of the Financial Crisis

The immediate effect of the financial crisis in 2008 was to increase the United States' dependence on countries with ready cash, in the form of large foreign currency reserves, who could refinance its banks and lend it the funds to restructure its economy. China features prominently among the exporters of energy and consumer products who head the list of such countries. Efforts by Congress to force China to revalue its currency against the dollar weakened. A bill introduced in the US Senate in May 2009 to review currency manipulation was last noted as being "unsure of proceeding." The financial crash, which had started in America, undermined the widely held belief that the United States had conducted its own economic affairs as well as it could have, and encouraged among Americans a degree of self-doubt previously missing from the debate on the American trade imbalances with China. America badly needed China's financial cooperation in maintaining China's existing lending to the American Treasury, and needed China to go on lending to support the American Government's efforts to stabilize its economy and its institutions. In any case, the rate of increase of America's trade deficit with China, which had ballooned from US$84 billion in 2000 to US$202 billion in 2005, had slowed, stabilizing in 2008 at US$266 billion, only US$10 billion more than 2007.[19] Meanwhile, American exports to China more than doubled between 2004 and 2008. The trade case against China was becoming less pressing.

The financial crisis brought about a sea change in the Sino–American relationship, creating a more even balance between the two sides, pushing month-to-month maintenance of the relationship up to the most senior levels of government, and broadening out the focus of cooperation from economic and security issues to a much wider range. At the London meeting on April 1, 2009, between the two leaders, President Obama made commitments to support the American economy and bring down the deficit, while President Hu committed to increase domestic demand and keep the Chinese economy on a track of sustainable fast growth. The economic discussions between the two countries would be led by US Treasury Secretary Tim Geithner and Wang Qishan, a senior vice-premier, while Hillary Clinton as Secretary of State and Dai Bingguo for China would lead the strategic discussions. The range of topics to be covered started with affairs of the greatest mutual interest—economic and terrorist affairs—but also included a wide range of other issues: law enforcement, climate change, culture, health, military affairs, and energy. Human rights were put at the back of the queue, defined as an issue to be discussed "as soon as possible."[20] The range of issues up for consideration balanced the Chinese interest in tapping American experience in high technology, education, and health with the American interest in economic, terrorist, and military issues. Both sides suddenly realized that they had a lot of things to talk about.

The G2?

Do these discussions herald a Group of Two or G2, whereby America and China decide a range of global issues on behalf of the rest of the world? In the Pacific, China and the United States are now the two dominant powers. With the United States able—through NATO, through its own multinationals such as General Electric, Exxon, and Microsoft, and through its bilateral relationships with Britain, France, and Germany—to exercise a stronger influence in Europe than any single European power, there is a case for thinking that the United States plus China could rule the world. America's preeminence as the sole superpower has been threatened by the crisis. Although the United States will remain the world's largest economy for at least the next two decades, the crisis has made it hear China's footsteps coming up behind it. Britain, which gradually lost its great power status through the first part of the twentieth century, after 1945 thought of its American diplomacy in the context of a "special relationship" with the United States which could maintain a British seat at the global top table. Comparable to the British situation post-1945 would be for the United

States to offer to share its power with China while it is still in a position to make such offers, and for China to accept its offer, feeling beholden to the US as a result.

But there are two problems with thinking of the Group of Two as a practical or likely option for running the world. The first is that a G2 ignores the European Union, the second largest economy after the United States. This simply makes a G2 impractical, because Europe is still big enough to make its inclusion necessary in any attempt at a global government. The second is that China has often stated its belief in multipolarity, a preference for the variety brought by each culture and country, and a dislike of a "one size fits all" approach to solving important global problems. China will certainly not want to limit itself to a relationship with the United States, preferring a multilateral approach to solving problems and advancing its interests. China's vast appetite for natural resources to drive its economy, and its search for export markets to help drive demand at home, have greatly expanded the development of China's relations with countries in Asia, Latin America, Africa, and Europe. These are places where the United States has been a dominant power for a generation and more, and so the American relationship is very important to China. But efforts by the US to turn the relationship into a kind of world government will not succeed.

When the United States finally recovers from the credit crisis, it will find that its relationship with China has changed permanently and enormously. The crisis has ended Washington's role as the place from which the world is unilaterally governed. The United States will not be able to take any important decisions in world affairs without China's support—not just in Asia, but around the world. Can the Sino–American relationship survive the tests which the future will bring? At present the relationship looks strong. The obvious damage to both parties, and to the world, if the relationship breaks down, appears to raise the stakes high enough to prevent serious rows. But China and the United States lack a long history of friendship. At its best, the United States stands for freedom, choice, and democracy. China's marvelous civilization cannot disguise the fact that it is a communist dictatorship and a police state, in which individual choice and freedom are limited for the vast majority of its population. In times of stress, people look to what they know best. Countries are no different. We must hope that a large common interest between China and America is sufficient to overcome their long history of mutual suspicion. President Obama's words in May 2009 announcing the appointment of the US Ambassador in Beijing were well chosen:

I'm making this appointment mindful of its extraordinary significance. Given the breadth of issues at stake in our relationship with China, this ambassadorship is as important as any in the world—because the United States will best be able to deal effectively with global challenges in the 21st century by working in concert with China. And that's why we're working with the government of China to stem the financial crisis that's devastated economies around the world and help lay a foundation for sustainable growth and lasting prosperity on both sides of the Pacific . . . There are few countries in the world with a past so rich or a future so full of possibility as China. With a vast population, a growing economy, and far-reaching influence, China will have a crucial role in confronting all the major challenges that face Asia and the world in the years ahead.[21]

Endnotes

1. Speech by Treasury Secretary Tim Geithner, "The United States and China, Cooperating for Recovery and Growth," Peking University, Beijing, June 1, 2009, US Treasury. http://www.ustreas.org.
2. Ibid.
3. *The Newshour* with Jim Lehrer, June 14, 1999.
4. "A Weakening of the West," Roger Altman, *Foreign Affairs*, January/February 2009.
5. Speech by Hillary Clinton to Asia Society, New York, February 13, 2009.
6. Adapted from edition of *Life*, March 1, 1943.
7. Deng's deathbed words have been reported to me by several Chinese independently of each other.
8. Wu Xinbo, *Washington Quarterly*, Autumn 2004.
9. Ibid.

10. Remarks by President Bill Clinton on China, Paul H Nitze School of Advanced International Studies, Washington, DC, March, 8, 2000.
11. US–China Trade Council.
12. Hearing before House Committee on Banking, Washington DC, July 25, 2001.
13. Ibid.
14. CNN, September 2001.
15. Testimony of Treasury Secretary John Snow before the Senate Committee on Banking, Housing and Urban Reform, October, 30, 2003.
16. "Schumer, Graham May Press for China Tariffs," Anjali Athavaley, *Washington Post*, July 29, 2005.
17. Remarks by Treasury Secretary, Henry M Paulson, on the International Economy. Washington DC, September 13, 2006.
18. Hearing before the Finance Committee, US Senate, March 29, 2006.
19. US–China Business Council.
20. Statement on April 1, 2009, bilateral meeting with President Hu Jintao, The White House Web site http://www.whitehouse.org.
21. Remarks by President Barack Obama in the nomination of Governor Jon Huntsman as Ambassador to the People's Republic of China, White House Web site http://www.whitehouse.org, May 16, 2009.

CHAPTER

7

China as Asian Leader

The strengthening of the Sino–American relationship as a result of the crisis has very important implications for China's role both in Asia and in the emerging world, two regions on which China's growing appetite for natural resources and energy depends. China's share of world oil consumption grew from 6.3 percent in 2000 to 9.5 percent in 2008.[1] The country depends on Angola, Saudi Arabia, and Iran as its major oil suppliers, and on countries in Africa and Latin America for its supply of metals. China's profile in Asia and the rest of the emerging world is critical to its security and long-term economic development.

In Asia, the crisis has raised the stakes for competition between the three pretenders to Asian leadership. We can already see clear signs of jockeying for position. How these intra-Asian tensions play out over the next decades of increasing Asian global influence is one of the most important issues to be managed, both for China and for the world. China has always been a force in Asia by virtue of its size and historic influence over the cultures of East and Central Asia, even when the country was poor and split by internal dissent. But today China's economy has become a powerful motor for Asian growth, and China has become a credible military force. With the backing of the United States, China can claim Asian leadership, a role that the two other major powers in Asia, Japan and India, naturally think of as theirs. A stronger China and a weaker United States gives rise to a number of questions in Asia. Will the Asian balance of power be upset? Can India and Japan live with a resurgent China which is backed by the United States? Is China now strong enough to resolve the Taiwan question peacefully? Can China use the United States' weakness to strengthen its position in energy-rich Central Asia, a region traditionally regarded by Russia as its strategic buffer and backyard? And if the Americans move closer to China, will that dissolve the strongest bond uniting Russia and China, that of opposition to American ambitions in Asia?

The Struggle for Leadership in Asia

China's role as Asia's trade hub has strengthened its power in Asia. Between 2000 and 2007, Asia's trade with China grew over four times, from US$274 billion in 2000 to US$1.19 trillion seven years later.[2] Malaysia, the Philippines, South Korea, Japan, Thailand, and Taiwan all run substantial trade surpluses with China, which is using its growing economic linkages with other Asian economies to strengthen its regional position and extend its influence. In 2007, the US and Europe were still the largest sources of demand for Asia's export-oriented economies. But over the next few years, as Western demand shrinks, and Chinese import demand starts to shift towards consumer products made in Asia, China will become the most important trade partner for Asia's large economies. For economies within Greater China, China is already the most important trade and regional partner by far. About 15 percent of China's trade in 2007 was with Taiwan, Hong Kong, and Macao. It is a natural process for China to reestablish itself in its traditional sphere of influence in Asia: to the south Vietnam, Laos, Cambodia, Burma, Thailand, Indonesia, and Malaysia; to the north Mongolia; and to the west Iran, Kazakhstan, and the other newly independent countries which lie between China and the energy-rich Caspian Sea. These countries have recognized Chinese religions and culture, including Confucianism, for many centuries. They respect China and look up to it, and have been China's trade partners for thousands of years.

But China's writ has never run in India, and it ceased having direct political influence on Japan many hundreds of years ago. China's relations in modern times with the other two major Asian powers, India and Japan, have been bad enough to make periods of friendliness appear as digressions from a natural state of hostility. Within living memory, events have occurred between China and the other two Asian powers that have given rise to strong feelings of dislike and mistrust on either side. The fundamental differences embedded in history and culture, which separate China from its two powerful neighbors, mean that there is no natural force of attraction, based on mutual admiration of each other's customs and culture, to offset the estrangements and hostilities of the recent past. Sustainable improvement in these relationships depends on whether the promise of shared economic opportunity which arises from China's and India's transformations can induce both sides to set aside old grievances and mistrust. China's rapid economic ascendancy since 2000, reinforced by China's permanent membership of the UN Security Council, has made it into the most powerful Asian country, and places it in a strong or even dominant position in both relationships, at least for the next few years. This may make it even harder for China to keep good relations with these other Asian powers, who each consider themselves, like China does, to be the natural leader of Asia.

Asia was protected from the financial effects of the 2008 crisis by the deep bank restructuring which occurred as a result of its own financial crisis a decade earlier. Although the collapse of demand in the developed economies in 2008 severely affected the most export-dependent Asian economies, which include Japan along with the small island economies of Singapore and Hong Kong, China and India remained relatively unscathed, due in large part to their own lack of financial sophistication, and the immaturity and inaccessibility of their domestic capital markets. Consequently, they have both gained in economic stature against a weakened developed world. Although the crisis has promoted China's position relative to almost every other major country because of its huge cash reserves, growth, and economic size, India, because of its obvious future potential as a fast-growing, large country, and Japan, because of its wealth, can both claim Asian leadership as much as China can.

Economic Competition and Interaction in Asia

A thumbnail comparison between the three countries gives some clues to the underlying economic issues which drive their relationships. Japan's population, at 128 million, is a fraction of India's 1.1 billion and China's 1.3 billion. But Japan's wealth, with a per head gross national income of US$37,790, is far greater than China's US$2,370, or India's US$950.[3] By contrast to Japan, which is one of the world's richest countries, China and India are both ranked by the World Bank as lower middle-income countries along with countries such as Armenia, Sri Lanka, Djibouti, and Egypt, with India achieving the apparently impossible task of being 2.5 times poorer than China, when measured on a national wealth per head basis. Aging, with its important wealth consequences, is another important issue differentiating the three countries. Although Japan is by far the richest of the three, it has the oldest population. In the 192-country aging survey compiled in 2007 by the Population Division of the UN, 27.9 percent of Japan's population was over 60, ranking the country the oldest in the world, with a median age of 42.9 years (meaning that, in 2007, half the population was above this age and half below). The equivalent retired ratios were 11.4 percent for China, making it 64th in the ranking, with a median age of 32.6, and 8.1 percent for India, making it 90th, with a median age of 24.3.[4] Aging has important consequences for economic growth, and it affects business and military strategies. In this case, it means that, as Japanese labor becomes scarce and expensive, and as the Japanese population shrinks, Japan is increasingly inclined to locate non-strategic manufacturing in China and other low-cost and convenient locations with plentiful populations. Japan also may be less likely to consider strategies depending on military intervention. India, on the other hand, with a much younger population than China, will not reach its full economic potential until much later in the 21st century, and may see itself as the real long-term future of Asia, as by 2050 its population will still be growing, while its two main competitors China and Japan will have shrinking populations. Towards the middle of the century, India's much greater relative youth could possibly increase the attractiveness of military strategies for dealing with disputes with China.

Japan is China's second largest trade partner and the largest major country source of foreign direct investment in China, while India's China trade, at US$39 billion overall in 2007, ranks some way down the list of countries that trade with China, between Thailand's and Britain's. Sino–Japanese trade in 2007 totaled US$236 billion, about one-fifth of overall Japanese trade, of which US$134 billion consisted of Japanese exports to China, and US$102 billion was Chinese exports to Japan.[5] Such a balance of the terms of trade against China, surprising to Western eyes, indicates the importance of China to Japan as a location for assembling high-value, high-technology products for sale to other markets. To protect manufacturing processes or other knowhow from prying Chinese eyes, and because it is more economical, Japan exports components to China which it makes in Japanese factories, using raw materials unobtainable in China such as special steels. Japan re-exports final products from China to their final destination, often America or Europe. China therefore benefits considerably from Japanese trade, although it runs a large deficit with Japan, as Japan effectively transfers part of its trade surplus with the West to China. Japan's economic linkage with China has come to play a critical role in its economy. Japan exported over three times more to China in 2007 than in 2000, and exports over those seven years rose as a proportion of its overall economy to 16 percent from 11 percent.[6] The fast expansion of China's economy since 2002 has been the largest factor by far in lifting the Japanese economy from its depressed state since the Japanese financial and real estate collapse of 1989–90. In the absence of the difficult internal changes needed to create stronger Japanese domestic demand, Japan has come to rely more and more on other countries' demand for its own products. The size of China's economy, which at US$4.4 trillion at the end of 2008 was only a little smaller than the Japanese economy itself, together with its growth rate averaging around 9 percent, has been a strong motor for Japan's own meager growth since the millennium.

India's trade with China increased after 2000 even more dramatically than Japan's, from US$2.9 billion to US$38.6 billion in 2007, and US$51.8 billion in 2008, an increase of more than 17 times in eight years.[7] One reason for the very sharp increase was that Chinese factories which were geared up for export to the United States found themselves from 2005 being squeezed by a rising Chinese currency, and started exploring other, less developed markets such as India more aggressively. Another reason was a growing trade in the raw materials for both countries' booming steel industries, with India buying coking coal from China, and China buying cheaper Indian iron ore to reduce dependence on its three major iron ore suppliers (CVRD in Brazil, Rio Tinto and BHP Billiton in Australia). Trade makes up about the same proportion, one-third, of both the Japanese and Indian economies. India's apparently modest trade in 2007 with China of US$39 billion simply reflects the much smaller size of India's economy relative to Japan's. Although India runs a trade deficit with China, unlike Japan, its Chinese trade relations are equally important to it.

China and India

Without the benefit of growing trade ties over the last decade, the difficult history of China's relations with the two other Asian powers is such that the position between them could have become very unstable. In India's case, the roots of the problem with China go back over 50 years. After Mao's accession in 1949, China invaded Tibet, a country which India wanted to keep as a wide buffer with China. India's Prime Minister Jawaharlal Nehru, realizing that India was not in a position to invade Tibet itself, accepted China's occupation as "de facto" and recognized Chinese sovereignty over Tibet, hoping to keep the mountainous border as a barrier to Chinese incursions into India. Nehru saw good relations between India and China as an essential basis for a stronger Asia, and encouraged the Tibetans to recognize Chinese sovereignty in 1951. In 1954 Nehru visited Beijing to sign an eight-year agreement with China covering the border region, which both sides agreed to consider as a no-go area. However, the construction of a Chinese road to link western China with India's rival Pakistan, which ran through Himalayan territory claimed by India, caused considerable upset in Delhi, and some border clashes occurred. Things got worse in 1959, when India refused China's request that India give up its claim to the Aksai Chin region on the Tibetan border in return for China ceding its claims in north-eastern India. In 1962, Chinese troops surprised and drove back Indian troops at the new Indian province of Arunachal Pradesh near Assam (called Southern Tibet by the Chinese), and further west near Ladakh in the Aksai Chin region, to create a new border between India and China-controlled Tibet, which India was forced to accept. Relations worsened through the 1960s as China began to split with the Soviet Union and further developed its friendship with Pakistan, while India took advantage of China's Soviet estrangement to become friends with the Soviets in 1971. Although the Soviet Union's invasion of Afghanistan in 1979 encouraged India and China to move closer, and relations have improved somewhat since, both sides remain mistrustful of the other.

As Hindu India and Muslim Pakistan have been at daggers drawn with each other since the partition of British India in 1947, and Pakistan's incursions into the disputed north-west Kashmir territory represent a constant problem for India, China's close relationship with Pakistan is a major irritant in the China–India relationship. Although the United States has intermittently supported Pakistan as a base for anti-Soviet or anti-terrorist campaigns, China has been Pakistan's steadfast ally since the 1950s and is the major power that Pakistan looks to for support above any other. Pakistan has cooperated closely with China in military affairs, uses Chinese fighters for its air force, receives substantial Chinese aid, and built its nuclear capability with Chinese knowhow. Pursuing a close relationship with Pakistan is a cost-effective way for China to force India to divert military strength away from its border with China and exert pressure on it. China's development and use of the Pakistani Port of Gwador, which lies close to the vital oil route of the Straits of Hormuz, and is one of several ports located in friendly Asian territories, which China uses to protect its shipping, is another illustration of the importance of Pakistan to China. The Indian–Chinese border in the Himalayas remains a bone of contention between the two Asia powers, and is a prime Asian hotspot along with the Taiwan straits and the border with North Korea. The

Indians maintain that China, while subsequently resolving all except one of its outstanding land border disputes with neighboring countries, has kept the territorial conflict with India alive, at times appearing to inflame the issue as a source of leverage over New Delhi.

Over the past two years, Chinese officials have publicly asserted Chinese claims to the entire northeastern Indian state of Arunachal Pradesh, which some Chinese military advisors and strategists refer to as Southern Tibet. Chinese forces have periodically engaged in small-scale cross-border encroachments, destroying Indian military bunkers and patrol bases in Ladakh and Sikkim. At the same time, China has been systematically constructing road and rail networks across the Tibetan plateau in ways that tilt the balance of forces along the contested frontier in China's favor; India has responded with infrastructure projects of its own, including roads and air fields, to enable military reinforcement of its border regions, but has failed to keep pace with its northern neighbor. China has also positioned large numbers of military and security forces on the Tibetan plateau, mainly with an eye on suppressing popular unrest.

One of the reasons for the persistence of the China–India border issue is the support given by the Indian government to the Dalai Lama, the religious and formerly the political leader of Tibet and head of the Tibetan Government. The Dalai Lama's escape from Tibet into India in 1959 brought him to the attention of the world's press, and he appeared on the cover of *Time* in that year, since when his government-in-exile have lived at Dharamsala in the province of Himachal Pradesh, in northeastern India under the protection of the Indian Government. The award of the Nobel Peace Prize in 1989 to the Dalai Lama further raised his profile, particularly in the United States, where two major films *Seven Years in Tibet* and *Kundun* were made about the Dalai Lama, both in 1997. The religious leadership exerted by the Dalai Lama over the Tibetan people and the focus that he provides worldwide to the Tibetan independence movement are a source of great irritation to China, which has adopted its own Tibetan leader, the Panchen Lama, and conducts propaganda campaigns inside China against the Dalai Lama and in support of its own Tibetan policies. India, which does not have many trump cards against China, holds onto the issue of the Dalai Lama and his exile inside India as an important bargaining counter with the Chinese.[8]

India's unresolved border problems with China are issues which continue to affect daily business between the two countries. An example is the dispute that arose early in 2009 between China and India over development assistance near the border. India, which has huge development and infrastructure needs just like China does, but lacks China's financial resources, is the largest borrower from the Asian Development Bank. India assembled a budget of US$2.9 billion for a funding application from the Asian Development Bank for a number of projects. One of these concerned flood engineering in disputed Arunachal Pradesh. Arunachal Pradesh lies within the basin of the Brahmaputra river, and is susceptible to flooding. In early 2009 India allocated US$60 million of its planned loan facility for flooding prevention work in the province. But when the loan came up for board approval at the bank meeting on March 26 and 27, 2009, China, the third largest shareholder after America and Japan in the Asian Development Bank, refused approval, on the basis that Arunachal Pradesh is a disputed territory.[9] This is the first time that China has escalated the border dispute with India to the level of a multinational institution. Although China indicated that it would approve the loan if the part relating to Arunachal Pradesh was withdrawn, India responded by withdrawing the whole loan application, asking the Asian Development Bank to negotiate a solution with China and attempting to persuade the other board members not to allow China to behave in this high-handed fashion. But in May 2009 the Bank informed India that it could not interfere in a matter of disputed territory between two states and invited India to pursue the issue directly with China. The dispute, which remains unsettled at the time of writing, demonstrates the rather one-sided nature of the relationship between China and India. India lacks China's hard cash and military resources, and so is forced to give way in a straight fight like this one. The dispute also illustrates China's increasing readiness to use multilateral institutions to exert its power.

India started its economic reform much later than China. Its economic development lags China's by at least a decade. Its economy still shows the signs of the Soviet central planning system that overtook it in the early 1970s, and it suffers from disunity and disorganization. Indian bureaucracy is notorious worldwide, and the country's infrastructure is antiquated. But India's recently high growth rates derive in part from something that China cannot easily imitate—a thriving private sector. A legal system which provides equal status before the law is an essential precondition for thriving private enterprises, who depend on the upholding of property rights for their ownership of intellectual property as well as real estate and other business assets. India, although bureaucratic and occasionally corrupt, has a legal system of which it is proud. It has also turned other relics of British rule, such as a strong accounting profession and a truly democratic political process, into systematic and powerful advantages for its economy and society. The Indian companies that have achieved global status are owned by families or individuals, while all the major multinational Chinese companies are State-owned. In India individual ownership rights can be protected in court. This is not always so in China, where the State exercises powerful control over all aspects of business and real estate ownership. A lot of the value that has been created by Indian companies has been gained by market penetration and brand building in a competitive environment, while much of the value in the large State-owned Chinese companies derives from monopoly rights inherited from their State parents. The strength of the Indian development model lies in its encouragement of private enterprise, which will probably prove in the long run to be a match for China's State-managed approach. The sustainability and efficiency of China's growth depends on creating greater competition within sectors and across the economy. This is not easily compatible with the domination of each sector by a few large, State-owned companies, which tend to stifle competition and bar new entrants.

However, the greatest barrier to close and sustainable cooperation between India and China is that the two peoples do not trust each other. There is little natural respect between the countries, in spite of the longevity of their cultures and the ancient shared religion of Buddhism which Chinese monks traveled to northern India to study and bring back to China. India feels it has as much entitlement as China to be number one in Asia, and resents China's position on the powerful UN Security Council. But for the next few years, China is the richer and more powerful of the two countries, and will hold the upper hand, particularly if the Sino–American relationship continues to strengthen.

India will not like taking orders from China, but until it develops wealth and hard power of its own, it has little choice but to play second fiddle to China in Asia. Meanwhile, the boom in Sino–Indian trade, which provides great economic benefits not just to China and India but to many other countries as well, is an increasingly strong force acting against the natural rivalry between the two countries.

China and Japan

Japan represents a different challenge to China, because Sino–Japanese relations are often difficult in spite of many shared characteristics and a long history of cultural influence. The factors that bind the two countries together are almost outweighed by the cultural and competitive differences. Japanese culture contains strong elements of Chinese influence. The historic Japanese city of Kyoto was built according to Chinese ideas of *feng shui* and modeled on the Chinese capital of that time, Chang'an. Other elements of Chinese culture brought to Japan by Japanese visitors to China included an imperial government, a writing system, Confucianism, Buddhism, and architecture. After 1860 and the restoration of the imperial monarchy, the Japanese, thinking of themselves as closer to the great powers than to Asia, modeled their society on the major foreign imperial powers.[10] Japan followed the United States in recognizing China in 1972, immediately after President Nixon's historic visit to China. Relations progressed, with the growth in trade between the two countries providing a strong common interest. China and Japan shared common views on many important issues affecting Asia in the 1980s and 1990s, including a dislike of Soviet involvement, particularly in Afghanistan.

For their part, the Chinese respect the fighting and business abilities of the Japanese, but remain deeply offended by the Japanese wartime legacy. China's strong objections to the atrocities committed by Japanese soldiers in China during the Second World War, shared by other East Asian countries such as Korea, are well known. China's insistence on full recognition of these atrocities, together with Japanese evasions of such recognition, remains a stumbling block between the two countries. The insistence of Japanese Prime Minister Junichiro Koizumi on observing the ritual of the annual visit to Japan's Yasukuni war shrine made for a cooling of relations, so that no senior Chinese leader visited Japan between 2000 and 2007. Both sides recognize the importance of maintaining good relations with the other, and Koizumi's successors have both tried to repair and improve the Chinese relationship, with state visits to Tokyo by Premier Wen Jiabao in 2007 and President Hu Jintao in 2008 marking a full resumption of relations.[11]

However, China's growth surge since 2000 has brought its economy close to Japan's in size, and Japan has become more nervous as China has started to flex its muscles. Points of tension between the two countries have multiplied. China has sought to block Japan's bid for a permanent seat on the UN Security Council. In April 2005, Chinese Premier Wen Jiabao told reporters on a trip to India:

Only a country that respects history, takes responsibility for history, and wins over the trust of peoples in Asia and the world at large can take greater responsibilities in the international community.[12]

The reaction of Japan to this Chinese putdown can be imagined.

The respective maritime rights of China and Japan in the South China Sea have also become an area of contention. On April 13, 2005, Japan gave the go-ahead on a US$1 billion project to drill for oil and gas in a disputed stretch of water west of Okinawa that both countries claim as their exclusive economic zone (EEZ). Chinese Foreign Ministry spokesman Qin Gang called Japan's decision "a serious provocation."[13] Japan, in response, claims China has repeatedly violated its EEZ around the Ryukyu Islands. In 2003, China began drilling in the Chunxiao and Duangqiao gas fields, which extend into territory claimed by Japan. Japan has also decided to make an issue of Taiwan, China's most sensitive spot, by making with the United States, on February 19, 2005, a joint agreement—the first of its kind—which stated that the status of Taiwan was a matter of mutual concern, thereby implying that China did not possess exclusive sovereign rights over Taiwan.

Until the post–credit crisis collapse in demand late in 2008, China was on the point of replacing the United States as Japan's largest trading partner. The shared economic and financial interest between the two countries makes a powerful argument for finding ways to live together. But Japan fears a strong China, whose new centrality to world finance is of major concern in Tokyo. As Japan's future remains deeply tied to the United States and its commitment to the alliance with Tokyo, Japan has to pay close attention to America's new friendliness with China and wonder if the US will continue to view Japan as its best friend in East Asia in future. Like India, Japan cannot be happy about the new Chinese ascendancy, but is not able to do much about it if the United States sides with China. Corporate Japan appears recently to have recognized the reality of a dominant China, and is redirecting its investment away from a suddenly much riskier developed world and towards an apparently less risky Asia, principally China. The trade links between the world's second and third largest economies look likely to continue to strengthen, with many large Japanese companies now considering investments in China. Japan appears to have little choice but to try to maintain good relations with China and pursue its economic and financial interests there for the foreseeable future. For its part, China will continue to use its increasing attraction as a destination for Japanese investment to insist on more open admissions by Japan of its wartime guilt, and in pursuit of its territorial claims in the South China Sea.

China and its Other Neighbors

Nowhere has China's new strength been more sharply felt than in the outlying areas of direct Chinese influence of Taiwan, Hong Kong, and Macao. All stand to be major beneficiaries of China's larger place in the post-crisis world. In 1992 the last Governor of Hong Kong, Chris Patten, arrived fresh from winning the British election for Prime Minister John Major to prepare the colony for handover to China in 1997 by strengthening its democratic institutions. The Chinese Government was nervous at the prospect of taking over responsibility for this prosperous colonial entrepot, whose success depended on the foreign virtues of openness and the rule of law. The British going-away present to the Chinese citizens of Hong Kong, of self-determination through democratically elected institutions, was understood by the Chinese Government as a deliberate attempt to rouse the passions of the Chinese citizens of Hong Kong ahead of the handover of power on July 1, 1997. Hong Kong temporarily became a battle ground for the hearts and minds of its Chinese residents. But China has always benefited more than anyone else from the prosperous development of Hong Kong. Although the Governor's democratic initiative in Hong Kong was met with a Chinese barrage of insults and criticism, China realized that in order to achieve its goal of maintaining Hong Kong's prosperity, it had to recognize the differences of the territory, and adopt a flexible approach to its government. Over 10 years later, Hong Kong—with its democratic institutions in place and more prosperous than ever—stands as a monument to Chinese and British pragmatism. Hong Kong's Chinese are either descended from mainland immigrants or immigrants themselves. It is natural for Hong Kong, and formerly Portuguese Macao, to view Beijing as their capital city, even if "the hills are high and the emperor is far away."[14]

Taiwan represents the largest challenge to China in Asia. As the home of the defeated Chinese nationalist party, the Kuomintang or KMT, Taiwan's existence as a separate state perpetuates the unresolved and epic pre-1949 struggle between the communists and the nationalists for control of China. The Taiwan Straits have represented one of the key flash-points in Asia for 60 years. America's support of Taiwan, derived from its wartime relations with the Chinese nationalists led by General Chiang Kai-Shek, and defined in the *Taiwan Relations Act of 1979*, does not recognize China's sovereignty over Taiwan, but commits America to providing Taiwan with weapons "of a defensive nature" without necessarily providing direct support in the event of a Chinese invasion. However, the possible need for America to assist Taiwan in its self-defense has "prompted the development and procurement of some of the US Navy's most expensive weapons systems."[15] China must assume that America would support the Taiwanese if it attacked Taiwan. Accordingly, China's ability to carry out an attack across the Taiwan straits, which is currently lacking, is one of the primary objectives underlying the buildup of the Chinese Navy. Taiwan's special relationship with Japan, who occupied the island from 1895 until 1945, is a point of friction in East Asian relations. The reinforcement in 2005 of the defense agreement between Japan and America, giving Japanese support to America's Taiwan policy, directly involves Japan in the delicate China–Taiwan relationship, which can only complicate and inflame it.

Establishing Beijing's sovereign right over the Chinese mainland means China ending unfinished business with the Kuomintang party based in Taiwan. China is as opposed to the pretensions of the Taiwanese to self-rule and their claims over mainland China as any regime is to pretenders who provide a rallying point for opposition to its rule. But the terms of any settlement agreeable to China would upset many native Taiwanese whose families were there before the nationalists arrived from the mainland after their defeat in 1949, and would also require a major shift in American policy towards Taiwan and East Asia. Finding a solution to the Taiwan problem, which for China only has one end—to bring Taiwan inside the People's Republic as a recognized province—is China's number one foreign policy issue and the foreign policy matter in which China has the strongest interest. The accession of a relatively pro-China Taiwanese premier in April 2008, in place of a regime opposed to China which supported Taiwanese independence, is assisting China to increase its influence inside Taiwan. The commencement of direct flights between Taiwan and the mainland and the arrival of mainland tourists in Taiwan are first steps in a Chinese campaign to gain Taiwanese support. The key factor in the evolution of Chinese relations with Taiwan is the attitude of the United States to Taiwan. America's new dependence on China as a result of the credit crisis may come to have a material effect on Taiwan's status, because complete American independence of action in matters of consequence to China has been compromised. America's dependence on China for financial support places China in a strong position to press for amendments to the American *1979 Taiwan Relations Act* and for a modification of American guarantees of support for the defense to Taiwan.

In addition to enabling it to intervene against the American Seventh Fleet in the Taiwan Straits and protect its vital shipping route to the Middle East, thereby reducing its reliance on the US Navy, China's current naval build up is designed to support China's extensive claims to the South China Sea, which contains hundreds of small islands which are claimed by China, Malaysia, the Philippines, Japan, and Vietnam. China seized the Paracel Islands in 1974, and there have been many clashes since then between China, Vietnam, and Japan. In addition to restoring what it sees as its ancient rights of sovereignty, China has an interest in protecting the extremely busy shipping routes that pass through the Malacca Straits into the South China Sea, which carry its oil imported from the Middle East and Africa, and its exports to Europe. Furthermore, high metal prices resulting from strong global growth have created new interest in undersea copper, and other mineral deposits which tend to run along cracks between the tectonic plates in the earth's crust. Such a crack runs north to south through areas of the South China Sea close to the Philippines and Japan. Much higher metal prices, resulting from periods of strong economic growth, would make undersea mineral deposits economic to exploit. China, which is already the world's largest consumer of metals, will need access to every source of minerals it can lay its hands on.

China shares a border with North Korea, and pursues a close relationship with its repressive regime which can only keep power by keeping on top in its long-running game of nuclear poker with the United States and the UN Security Council. China's primary interest has been in preventing a regime collapse in Pyongyang which would cause millions of starving Koreans to cross the border into China in search of food and shelter, but China's emergence since the crisis has changed its approach to the North Korean problem, highlighting its international responsibilities as an important global leader as against its own domestic concerns. Moreover, South Korea is one of China's most important trading partners. As noted earlier, China's influence with North Korea is of great strategic importance to the United States. The change in China's approach to North Korea became apparent when the Security Council unanimously passed Resolution 1874 in early June 2009, which placed tough new sanctions on Kim Jong-il's regime, in response to North Korea's missile test and rejection of six-nation talks in May. China became involved in drawing up the sanctions package against North Korea, and privately indicated its frustration with the North Korean regime. China has a delicate balancing act to play with North Korea. It has to keep talking to the regime so that it can continue to exert "friendly" influence, but at the same time it has to burnish its credentials as a newly paid-up and responsible senior member of the global leadership team. The likelihood is that it will find ways of bringing Kim Jong-il's regime back from the brink.

The credit crisis has also impacted favorably on China's position in resource-rich Central Asia, an area of increasing economic and strategic significance. The countries lying along the ancient Silk Road, which for two thousand years and more linked China with the markets of the West, all have very long histories of relations with China, based on trade and a recognition of China's wealth and cultural supremacy. Now that the Central Asian region has become a strategically important global center for energy production, its long-standing and generally friendly relations with China provide a platform for steady Chinese expansion into the region. Russia maintains a strong proprietorial interest in the region following the collapse of the Soviet Union in 1990. The Shanghai Group formed by China and Russia in 1996, later the Shanghai Cooperative Organisation, was originally aimed at providing a diplomatic vehicle for the ironing-out of border disputes, but has now extended its activities to joint efforts against Islamic terrorism and provides China with a means to access the region's vast oil and gas reserves—in competition with American and European interests—by providing investment and other forms of assistance. The Shanghai Cooperative Organisation is one of several points where China and Russia share common interests. Opposition to American global hegemony united Joseph Stalin and Mao Zedong after 1949. Today it remains the strongest force bringing the two countries together. In the 1970s the Soviet Union's economy was roughly four times larger than China's, but today this position is reversed. Against the background of China's dramatic rise, although relations between China and Russia since 2000 have improved under Presidents Vladimir Putin and Hu Jintao, any perception of American weakening as a result of the credit crisis may remove one of the main reasons for Russian–Chinese friendship. Although China is a large buyer of oil, other natural resources, and weapons from Russia, China today needs Russia less than Russia needs China and its hard currency. Both would probably trade in the other for a solid relationship with the West.

The region west of China has become important to China because it is becoming, once again, an important trade route; 2007 saw the volume of Chinese trade conducted through its western province of Xinjiang rise by over 60 percent to US$18.4 billion, of which two-thirds were exports. According to 2007 data, China trades with 148 countries through Xinjiang, and this route is its main contact point with Iran and Pakistan.[16] Once the Kashgar–Osh–Andijan railroad, which runs along one of the old Silk Road routes, is completed, China will have a direct route to Central Asia and Europe which does not pass through Russia. China cooperates with all the energy-rich independent countries in the region, including Kazakhstan, Uzbekistan, Turkmenistan, and Azerbaijan (see Figure 7.1 for the size of energy reserves).

China's relationship with Iran is an ancient one, including strong trade links along the Silk Route, as well as important cultural exchanges. There is a natural cultural affinity between China and Iran based on their ancient civilizations, to add to the strong trading relationship and Iran's huge energy reserves. Iran, between Iraq and Afghanistan, bordering the energy-rich Caspian Sea and with a population of nearly 70 million, occupies a strategically vital location in Central Asia. The Iran–China relationship is becoming a core political axis which helps to assure

Figure 7.1   Central Asian Oil Reserves

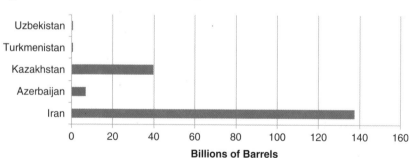

Source: British Petroleum Statistical Energy Survey 2009

China's energy needs, as well as ensuring stability in the region and countering the American presence in Iraq and Afghanistan. Iran, which possesses 16 percent of world gas and 11 percent of world oil reserves, second in the world only to Saudi Arabia, provides about 15 percent of China's total oil imports, also supplies China with liquefied natural gas, and is a major buyer of Chinese exports.[17] Overall trade between China and Iran has grown at an annual rate of 40 percent in the last few years, to a level of about US$29 billion in 2008.[18] With its veto on the Security Council, China is able to block US and European efforts to isolate Iran as it pursues its nuclear program. This affects American relations not only with Iran, but with Israel. American diplomacy is beginning to shift in recognition of the impossibility of outlawing Iran in the face of firm Chinese support. The pressure on Israel from the United States to recognize and realize a two-state solution to the Palestinian problem has been affected by the need for the United States to come to terms with China's strong links with Iran.

China's economic growth, demand for energy, and huge capacity to provide poorer countries with inexpensive consumer products is drawing other Asian countries into its orbit like a magnet, enabling China to counter territorial disputes and other local disagreements, and extend its influence throughout the region. Saudi Arabia, now China's first or second largest oil supplier (a role it alternates with Angola) has recently moved towards China, assisted by China's readiness to invest in refineries which can handle its heavy, sulphurous oil which cannot easily be sold elsewhere.[19]

American naval and economic power has long held the key to Asia, and continues to protect China's vital shipping routes. But the credit crisis has weakened the American grip and increased the support of the United States for China, reducing the influence of America's traditional ally in the region, Japan, and potentially undermining the traditional alliance between China and Russia based on opposition to the United States. Instances of China forcing local issues in its favor are beginning to crop up all over Asia. Taiwan, always the most important foreign issue for China, is top of China's Asian agenda, and China will seek to use its new leverage with the US to weaken support for Taiwan and force the issue. Access to natural resources and the recognition of Chinese sovereignty are the two other principles which will drive the extension of China's Asian influence. China is now in a position where it can redefine the map of Asia in its favor. With the Americans hamstrung by their dependence on Chinese finance, India and Japan have no option but to yield to Chinese assertiveness, while China's growing economy provides a juicy carrot for closer cooperation. A gradual replacement of American by Chinese influence in Asia is inevitable over the course of the next two or three decades, the natural consequence of China's growth and the new weakness of the United States.

Endnotes

1. BP Statistical Review of World Energy, June 2009.
2. *China Statistical Yearbook* 2008. National Bureau of Statistics of China.
3. World Bank Web site http://www.worldbank.org.
4. "China's Long March to Retirement Reform—The Graying of the Middle Kingdom Revisited," Richard Jackson, Keisuke Nakashima and Neil Howe, Center for International & Strategic Studies and The Prudential Foundation, Washington DC, US, 2008.
5. *China Statistical Yearbook* 2008. National Bureau of Statistics of China.
6. Ibid.
7. Ibid, http://www.atimes.com, February 20, 2009.
8. I am indebted to Arun Singh, OBE for valuable insights and information concerning the history and current status of India's relationship with China.
9. *The Indian Express*, May 17, 2009.
10. Lord Trenchard gave me the benefit of his great experience and knowledge of Japan. Some of my remarks about Japan are based on his comment. The chapter also benefited greatly from the readiness of Dr. John Villiers to share his considerable knowledge of East Asia.
11. "Strained Ties Between China and Japan," Lionel Beehner and Preeti Bhattacharji, US Council for Foreign Relations, March 14, 2008.
12. *China Daily*, April 13, 2005.
13. Ibid.
14. Common Chinese saying.

15. Unpublished thesis, "The US Navy and the PLA Navy: Linchpin of the US Military Strategy Towards the People's Republic of China," Lt Cmdr Aron Buckles, Quantico, Virginia, 2006.

16. "The Central Asian Policy of the People's Republic of China," Ablat Khodzayev in Central Asian Perceptions of China, *The China and Eurasia Forum Quarterly*, vol. 7, no. 1, February 2009.

17. *People's Daily*, May 2009.

18. "The Central Asian Policy of the People's Republic of China," Ablat Khodzayev in Central Asian Perceptions of China, *The China and Eurasia Forum Quarterly*, vol. 7, no. 1, February 2009.

19. *The Vital Triangle: China, the United States, and the Middle East*, Jon B Alterman and John Garver, Center for Strategic & International Studies, Washington DC, 2008.

CHAPTER

8

China and the Emerging World

In the emerging world, America's post-crisis financial embarrassment and new state of dependency has fundamentally changed the calculus underpinning the global web of superpower influence.

Until 1990, a poor, strategically located country dependent on a steady stream of aid, such as Ethiopia or Cuba, could choose between two superpowers, either of which would provide financial and other kinds of assistance, in return for the country signing up, at least nominally, to their values and culture, and giving them permission to station military hardware and troops on their soil. With the weapons of money, technical assistance, and military hardware, the Cold War was fought as fiercely in the emerging world as in the developed one. But 1990 and the fall of the Soviet empire removed the choice. For a decade, America and its allies exercised unlimited global influence. Since 2000, China's increasing wealth, need for global involvement, demand for natural resources, and subtle diplomacy has again provided emerging countries with a powerful and attractive potential partner, one which offers the opportunity to develop their economies through trade as well as other kinds of assistance, but with no preconditions to be met or value systems to be subscribed to. The fate of the emerging world depends on the most powerful and richest countries. The actions and attitudes of poorer countries represent a barometer which is highly sensitive to changes in the global power climate. Nowhere has the change in the global power balance become more evident than in the emerging country clientele of the superpowers.

China's Post-Revolution History with the Emerging World

China's involvement in the emerging world was based on the fact that from 1949 until the 1970s, most countries followed America's lead in recognizing Taipei, not Beijing, as the capital city of the Chinese mainland. Smaller countries followed their example. The main incentive for China's foreign policy under Mao was the pursuit of international recognition of the communist regime. The People's Republic pursued its international legitimacy wherever it could bring influence to bear, and evolved a strategy that could allow it to exercise influence, despite its poverty and isolation. Mao divided the world into three. The first world comprised the two superpowers: the United States and the Soviet Union. The second world included existing major powers and developed countries such as Britain, France, Germany, and Japan. The others, which he called the third world, were poor countries concentrated in Africa, Latin America, and Asia, almost all of which in the 1950s and early 1960s had colonial memories and relationships, if indeed they had achieved independence by then. Mao focused his foreign policy on third world countries, to form a socialist group which could be united by its recognition of the People's Republic of China and opposition to the United States, and thereby exercise global influence. The strategy was primarily aimed at isolating Taiwan and gaining support for China's recognition. The slogans "peaceful coexistence" and "mutual benefit," which we associate with China's diplomacy today, were not evident 50 years ago. In a world which he saw as being divided into two camps, Mao "leant to one side."[1] Until China turned in on itself, and for a time became isolated from the outside world as the murderous madness of Mao's Cultural Revolution took hold, Mao's third world strategy actively sought socialist partners, such as Cuba, who could share China's Leninist ideology and join in the struggle against American imperialism.

Nixon's visit to Beijing in 1972 and China's entry into the United Nations in the previous year encouraged most major countries, who had not already recognized the People's Republic, to do so. By 1980 China had established diplomatic relations with all the G7 countries. Most other countries followed. Today, only a handful of countries—none in Africa, and only Paraguay in Latin America—still recognize Taiwan as the sovereign ruler of the Chinese mainland, a privilege for which Taiwan has to pay dearly. Today, although it is still important for China to attract widespread external support for its policy of isolating Taiwan internationally, recognition for the Beijing regime has been replaced as the principal force behind China's policy in the resource-rich emerging world by China's own development needs. China is still at an early stage of its physical development, but is already the world's largest or second largest consumer of every natural resource. Its needs will continue to dominate world commodity markets for decades to come. Emerging countries, whose markets and treasuries have been swollen by China's huge purchases of commodities, are taking up much of the slack in demand for Chinese consumer products created by the shrinkage of Western markets arising from the credit crisis and its associated recession.

China's distinctive approach to poor countries is based on its own status as a once poor and unrecognized country. It was articulated by the People's Republic's first foreign minister, the famous right-hand man to Mao and Long Marcher Zhou Enlai, on visits to Mali and Sudan in 1963 and 1964. Zhou Enlai's approach was based on China's view of itself not as a donor but a partner to third world countries, and emphasized the crucial need to respect the sovereignty of other countries. Zhou said assistance provided by China to another poor country had no conditions attached to it. It should not place any burden on recipient countries or create a dependency, but rather should lead to quick results for the country concerned in terms of income generation and capital creation.

Chinese experts providing technical assistance to other countries should not enjoy any privileges, but have the same standard of living as the inhabitants of the country to which they were providing assistance.[2]

China and Africa

As the local director of a large international aid agency in one of the biggest African countries, Sudan, in the early 1980s, I had personal experience of China's approach to third world cooperation. In the late 1970s China sent a large group of Chinese engineers to build a railway to connect landlocked Khartoum, the capital of Sudan, with Port Sudan, 1,200 kilometers away on the Red Sea. The Chinese camp in the north Sudanese desert lay about 50 kilometers from the eastern border town of Gedaref, next to Ethiopia, the home of many thousands of refugees who had fled the fierce factional fighting in Ethiopia, and the base for relief agencies, including my own. Every week a team of doctors and other aid workers from agencies based in Gedaref used to visit the Chinese railway workers' camp to play basketball and eat supper. We were always impressed by their irrigation system, which channeled the water they used for washing and cooking into their vegetable garden, before being allowed to run off. They kept chickens and goats, and as a result our meals always contained plenty of fresh vegetables and meat, which in that part of Sudan were expensive, and when out of season were difficult to find. Although our team—consisting of North Americans, Europeans, and Antipodeans—always won our games, being on average a foot taller than the Chinese, and we were unable to converse with our hosts, they seemed unworried by either problem and usually invited us for a rematch the following week. The cheerfulness and resilience of these Chinese living in the desert many thousands of miles from home impressed us, and gave an excellent account of their homeland, a country which at that time none of us knew.

Since the 1950s, this tale from Sudan has been replicated thousands of times all over Africa, Asia, and Latin America, and has encouraged emerging countries to think of China as a friend and partner, and not as a competitor or a master. The view taken by emerging countries of all the Western European countries, particularly the major colonial powers Britain and France, is inevitably colored by the servant–master relationship employed by the imperial powers to control their colonies. In the 45 years between the end of the Second World War and the fall of communism, the American third world policy was largely dictated by its global struggle with the Soviet Union. Since 1990 and the collapse of the Soviet communist system, the strategic interests of the United States have been the factors underpinning American relations with emerging countries. The invasions of Afghanistan and Iraq, both emerging countries par excellence, were determined entirely by the American domestic agenda. The conditions attached to US aid include observing human rights, protecting the environment, promising not to send US military personnel to the International Criminal Court, not assisting current or former terrorists, and not using US-provided equipment for anything other than its stated purpose.[3] By contrast, China's no-strings approach increases its attractiveness to many emerging country regimes, including those who want to reduce dependency on America, such as Brazil and Venezuela, and outcasts who do not wish to be subject to Western rules, such as Sudan and Myanmar. Even countries who enjoy excellent relations with the West, such as South Africa, welcome China's markets and the new options for development and cultural exchange that China brings. In Africa, Latin America, and Asia, many emerging countries pursue relations both with China and the United States. In other cases, such as Zimbabwe or Sudan, where the US and its allies disapprove of the government's policy and have left the country, China is left with a free hand to pursue its own strategic interests involving oil in Sudan and rare strategic metals such as vanadium and chromium in Zimbabwe.

In November 2006, China invited 48 of Africa's 52 countries to Beijing for a summit with the title "Friendship, Peace, Development and Cooperation." China went out of its way to treat its African guests as equals. During the three days of the summit, each of the 41 African heads of state or other senior representatives of the countries present had a one-to-one meeting with Chinese President Hu Jintao. Friendly cooperation, mutual benefit, and respect, not aid, were the slogans. Even Burundi, with US$12 million of trade with China, was treated as an equal and had its own face-to-face meeting with the Chinese President. A report in the Chinese media of the meeting between China and Burundi read:

The two countries respect each other politically and treat each other on an equal footing and work in close cooperation in international affairs and have carried out fruitful cooperation in areas such as trade, economic and social development.[4]

The summit produced agreements signed between 12 Chinese firms and various African governments and companies, and Hu Jintao's pledge to offer US$5 billion in loans and credit followed.

The joint declaration that ended the summit announced a strategic partnership and "action plan" that laid out cooperation between China and African countries in the economy, international affairs, and social development. It read:

We propose to enhance South–South cooperation and North–South dialogue to promote balanced, coordinated and sustainable development of the global economy.[5]

The deals reached included commitments from China to build expressways in Nigeria, lay a telephone network in rural Ghana, and erect an aluminum smelter in Egypt. The Ethiopian Foreign Minister at the time, Seyoum Mesfin, rejected criticism that China was doing business with African countries without regard to governance or human rights and was bolstering governments that the West has tried to isolate, maintaining instead that the relationship was helping to fight poverty in Africa and that the continent needed cooperation without political conditions. "This has nothing to do with turning a blind eye to the predicaments of Africa," he said at a news conference. "It is to promote human values, including human rights. Is not the right to development a human rights issue?" His colleague Tsegab Kebebew, a senior official in Ethiopia's foreign ministry, was still enthused about the China relationship one year after the summit. "This is a new strategic partnership. There is no colonial history between Africa and China, so they are well received here. There is no psychological bias against the Chinese."[6]

The West does not share the enthusiasm of African countries for China's pragmatic, business-led approach to resource-rich countries which are often ruled by dictators, where corruption runs unchecked and where roads, schools, and hospitals remain unbuilt. A piece in Britain's popular broadsheet *The Daily Mail* by reporter Andrew Malone in July 2008, entitled "How China is Taking Over Africa and Why the West Should be Very Worried," gave a flavor of this view:

Confucius Institutes (state-funded Chinese cultural centres) have sprung up throughout Africa, as far afield as the tiny land-locked countries of Burundi and Rwanda, teaching baffled local people how to do business in Mandarin and Cantonese . . . From Nigeria in the north, to Equatorial Guinea, Gabon and Angola in the west, across Chad and Sudan in the east, and south through Zambia, Zimbabwe and Mozambique, China has seized a vice-like grip on a continent which officials have decided is crucial to the superpower's long-term survival . . . According to one veteran diplomat, China is easier to do business with because it doesn't care about human rights in Africa—just as it doesn't care about them in its own country. All the Chinese care about is money. Nowhere is that more true than Sudan . . . through its supplies of arms and support, China has been accused of underwriting a humanitarian scandal.[7]

China's official view is that a country is free to decide on how it governs itself and how it spends its money, and China does not interfere in internal matters. But this apparently reasonable argument is difficult to stomach when applied to some of Africa's worst and most corrupt dictators. Since 1987, Robert Mugabe has been President of Zimbabwe, a country which was highly prosperous and a major food exporter as little as 25 years ago, but which is now bankrupt and whose population hovers on the edge of starvation, with disease and dire poverty widespread. Zimbabwe possesses rare metals which are required for the production of special-purpose steels for jet engines and other military and civil uses. These include vanadium, cobalt, and chromium. It also has lithium which is needed for the manufacture of mobile, computer, and electric car batteries, as well as platinum, gold, coal, copper, nickel, iron ore, and asbestos. All of these resources are highly attractive to China, which sees in Zimbabwe a country where it can obtain scarce commodities at a low price. Consequently China supports Mugabe with money, weapons, and military personnel, in return for mining concessions. No country will trade with the Zimbabwe regime except China, which is able to do extremely good business because of Zimbabwe's reliance on the money, troops, and weapons that it supplies.

Some argue that Beijing's approach is not significantly different from how any other country pursues its interests. "The United States is highly selective about who we're moral about," says David A Kang, a professor of government at Dartmouth College in New Hampshire, "We support Pakistan, Egypt, Saudi Arabia—huge human-rights violators—because we have other strategic interests. China's not unique in cutting deals with bad governments and providing them arms."[8] America's Central Intelligence Agency has long had a reputation for cynical foreign interventions, including the support of public enemy number one Saddam Hussein against Iran when American access to Iraqi oil appeared threatened. Neither would many actions carried out longer ago by Britain and the other imperial powers bear examination from a moral standpoint. Perhaps the historical record of international relations over the years justifies a neutral stance on the morality of China's foreign policy.

However, China's influence on Africa has improved the wellbeing of millions of Africans. This is marked by a dramatic and beneficial increase in Africa's trade, including vastly increased exports of oil and other natural resources to China, and rising imports of Chinese consumer goods, particularly by Africa's larger and more prosperous economies Algeria, South Africa, and Egypt. Between 2000 and 2007, China–Africa trade grew almost seven times (see Figure 8.1), to a total of US$74 billion, representing a huge increase to many poor African countries, although accounting for only 2 percent of China's trade.[9] China has overtaken former African colonial powers Britain and France to become Africa's second largest trade partner after the United States. African oil exports make up the largest part of the increase of Africa's exports to China,

Figure 8.1   The Growth of China's Trade with the Emerging World 2000–07

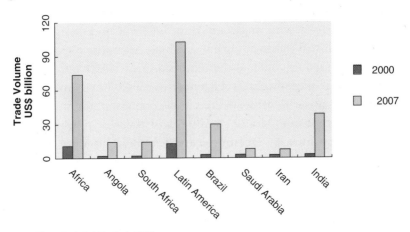

Source: *China Statistical Yearbook* 2008

with Angola, China's number one oil supplier ahead of Saudi Arabia, increasing the value of its oil exports seven times since 2000. China runs trade deficits with the poorer resource-rich African countries, whose markets are too undeveloped to absorb Chinese consumer products. But African imports of Chinese consumer goods have also increased dramatically, and the continent's ability to absorb Chinese exports is increasing even faster than China's hunger for natural resources. Following years of Chinese trade deficits with Africa, the African appetite for Chinese consumer products is moving the terms of trade in favor of China. Nevertheless, China's continuing hunger for African resources will tend to limit the increase of China's surplus with Africa. China's overall trade surplus with Africa in 2007 was US$939 million, only 1 percent of overall Chinese–African trade, with the oil-exporting, undeveloped countries of Sudan, Equatorial Guinea, Libya, Gabon, the Congo, and Angola all running substantial trade surpluses with China.[10]

China's involvement in emerging countries stretches much further than buying commodities and shipping container-loads of consumer goods in return. Its need to recycle its massive hard currency surpluses and its enormous appetite for natural resources of every kind are building up an unstoppable Chinese drive to invest overseas. So far, China's efforts to secure significant stakes in resource enterprises in America, Australia, and other developed countries have foundered on the unwillingness by developed countries to countenance ownership of their resources by a major Asian power who might still turn out to be an enemy. Chinese retaliation against Western companies wishing to acquire majority stakes in Chinese companies, such as the rebuff of Coca-Cola's bid to acquire China's largest juice producer Huayuan in early 2009, may send an important signal to developed countries, but does not immediately solve China's problem. African countries with valuable resources which welcome Chinese equity investment are extremely attractive to China. China's African initiative is therefore aimed at developing Africa as a target for investment by Chinese corporates. In June 2007 China's State Council established the China–African Development Fund (CADFund) as the institutional vehicle to manage the US$5 billion of investment and credits which President Hu Jintao had announced earlier at the 2006 China–African summit in Beijing. The CADFund is financed by the China Development Bank, which exists to pursue national Chinese strategies, and which is controlled directly by the State Council. By early 2009 the Fund had completed most of its first phase of investments up to a value of US$1 billion, nearly two years earlier than originally planned. It announced in March 2009 that it was going to add a further US$2 billion of capital, to be available immediately to take advantage of opportunities created by the sudden disappearance of Western investors as a result of the credit crisis. The Fund's Web site describes its role as follows:

CADFund is a pioneering move in the process of mutually beneficial cooperation between China and Africa. It remedies the gap under the traditional model of free aid and loans. And without increasing the debt burden to African countries, through the market-oriented operation to achieve the sustained and healthy self-development. CADFund, as a thruster, will fully use for reference from the international PE investment fund mode and the direction of economic development of African countries, to play a role in promoting the partnership, to guide and support more Chinese enterprises to develop the direct investment, to promote market-oriented economic development, to improve the people's livelihood for African regions by investment and fund advisory services and other ways.[11]

Also in March 2009 the Fund chose the most developed African country, South Africa, to establish its first representative office in Johannesburg. In the first two years of CADFund's life, investments have been made in agriculture ventures in Ethiopia, Malawi, and Mozambique, in a share of a US$450 million power station in Ghana, and in Egyptian, Nigerian, and Mauritian industrial zones. The Fund has also invested in Zimbabwe. The US$400 million it has spent so far "will drive Chinese enterprises to make investments of more than $2 bn."[12] Recently, however, one of China's State-owned railway construction companies was forced to suspend operations in Nigeria, when the Nigerian transport ministry took over control of a project which had been signed just before the African summit in Beijing in 2006 to renovate the long north–south railway line. A new administration in Nigeria justified the suspension on the grounds that the contract was "inflated," and stated they would take 90 days to redefine the project, for which China had received the promise of a block of oil exploration rights.[13] Problems have also been encountered in the Congo with China's agreement to invest US$9 billion in roads and railways, in return for majority stakes in mining rights. China's investment expansion into Africa is bound to encounter the same delays, cancellations, and terminations experienced by every other foreign investor in the continent. But China needs the resources, and African countries need the cash and the investment, and so the Chinese presence in Africa will continue to develop.

China and Latin America

China's penetration of Africa has been matched by its recent activities in Latin America, the backyard of the United States. China's historical direct contacts with Africa were limited to a visit to Mombasa and Malindi on Africa's east coast around 1430 by the famous Chinese admiral Zheng He. But for several centuries from 1575 China sent 20 or 30 ships a year across the Pacific to trade with Latin American countries, selling silk, gunpowder, and jewellery, and bringing back wine, olive oil, and soap. These contacts were suspended from the time that all Chinese external trade stopped in the early nineteenth century, until the late 1950s when Mao started looking for third world countries to form alliances with. The development of American global power and hegemony after the Second World War created an incentive for independent countries in Latin America to distance themselves from their powerful neighbor. Mao was immediately attracted to the socialist revolution in Cuba, as Castro publicly cut ties with Taiwan in 1959 and attached himself to the People's Republic. In 1960 Chinese Foreign Minister Zhou Enlai told Castro that "if necessary, China will furnish all necessary assistance to the Cuban people in their fight for freedom."[14] Cuba became the first country in the Americas to recognize Beijing over Taipei. Rallies throughout China were organized during the Cuban missile crisis to support Cuba in its fight against American imperialism.

Although Mao used disputes between the United States and countries in Central and Latin America as an excuse in his speeches in the 1960s to inveigh against American imperialism, it was only when a socialist regime was elected in Chile under President Salvador Allende in 1970 that another country in the region actually recognized China. Two years later in 1972, President Richard Nixon's China visit encouraged other Latin American countries to follow Cuba and Chile. By 1975, Peru, Mexico, Argentina, and Brazil had all broken ties with Taiwan and established relations with Beijing. When China badly needed friends after the brutal suppression of Chinese students in Tiananmen Square in 1989, Deng Xiaoping used Mao's policy of making friends with third world countries, but with a variation. While he respected old socialist ties with countries such as Cuba, he did not require that China's third world friends follow socialism, and looked for relations with countries of a different ideology to China, preaching mutual understanding and non-interference. In 1990, the year after Tiananmen, Deng sent Chinese President Yang Shangkun to visit Argentina, Mexico, Brazil, Uruguay, and Chile, with the message that China wanted to increase its ties with Latin America through high-level contacts, cultural exchanges, and trade. It took another decade before Jiang Zemin's visit to Venezuela, Cuba, Brazil, Chile, Uruguay, and Argentina in 2001 really got things going between China and Latin America. His visit coincided with the midair collision, mentioned earlier, between a Chinese air force pilot and an American spy plane off China's south coast, as a result of which the Chinese pilot died and the American plane was forced to land and was taken hostage by the Chinese. The Americans noticed that although Jiang clearly took the incident very seriously, he did not immediately return to China. From this they deduced that Latin America was of high importance to China, and started to examine the nature of China's strategy in the region.

They found that Jiang Zemin's visit was intended as a big step in building Sino–Latin American relations. His approach stemmed from existing concepts, namely Mao's idea of a united socialist third world, varied by Deng to include diverse political ideologies and emphasize mutual economic benefit. The enormous recent expansion in China's influence in Latin America stems from Jiang's earlier visit, and has been reinforced since by many visits by senior Chinese leaders to Latin American countries. In 2004 Hu Jintao visited Argentina, Brazil, Chile, and China's traditional regional ally Cuba on his way to the APEC meeting. These countries responded to Hu's invitation to expand economic and political ties by granting China the special designation of Market Economy Status, entitling China to relief from World Trade Organization anti-dumping regulations, no small matter, and underpinning the fast penetration of China's exports to the region. Hu made another trip in 2008 to Peru and Costa Rica on his way to the G20 summit in November 2008, just after the release of China's White Paper on Latin America which marked the importance of the region.

Both Africa and Latin America are resource-rich continents and highly attractive to China, which has greatly increased imports from both in recent years. In 1994 China was Latin America's 12th largest trade partner. Now it ranks second behind the United States. The capacity of Latin America's relatively developed economies—such as Argentina, Chile, Brazil, Mexico, Venezuela, Peru, and Panama—to absorb Chinese exports has made China's Latin American trade develop even faster than China's trade with Africa, where only South Africa has a large wealthy middle class which can buy China's consumer goods in large quantities. At US$11.4 billion, China's exports to Brazil in the calendar year 2007 were 2.4 times larger than in 2005. But in 2007 Brazil, which has the world's largest and purest deposit of iron ore and is also a large soya bean producer, still sold US$7 billion more to China than it bought from China.[15] China also ran large trade deficits with Chile and Peru (both producers of copper and its by-products gold and silver) and Argentina (the world's largest beef producer). But after soaring Chinese metal imports had tilted the terms of trade heavily in Latin America's favor between 2000 and 2005, a recent surge of Chinese exports to Latin America has brought the trade position between the two continents back into rough balance. As with Africa and other emerging countries, China's strong appetite for resources, which has lifted the prices of oil and other resources to a new, much higher plateau, and its inexpensive consumer products, which increase the standard of living of poor households, have greatly benefited both the economies and the populations of Latin America and reduced greatly their dependence on trade with North America. Some emerging countries—such as Mexico, who have depended on trade in manufactures rather than in commodities, but have lower productivity than China—have suffered from China's expansion. These are being forced to find new sources of competitive advantage. But even for these countries, China's multi-faceted development does present economic opportunities as well as threats.

As in Africa, China has started to make some substantial investments in infrastructure in Latin America, usually directed at the natural resource sector which is of particular Chinese interest. And as in Africa, the abandonment of particular countries by America and its allies, for example Argentina following its financial default in 2001, gives China an opportunity to access opportunities on extremely favorable terms and develop a strong and lasting relationship with a particular country. In November 2004 China committed to invest US$19 billion in Argentina.[16] Most of this money was earmarked for expansion of the Argentinian railway system, and similar infrastructure projects which would facilitate extraction and shipment of the country's mineral resources. A direct consequence of the 2008 credit crisis was that in October 2008 China was allowed to join the Inter-American Development Bank (IDB), after years of being rebuffed by the Bank's principal shareholder America, on the grounds that America did not want to encourage China's involvement in its own backyard. Membership of the IDB makes it much easier for China to gain access to good infrastructure projects of real significance to the countries concerned, which it can finance at much lower risk than if it intervened financially on a bilateral basis with the relevant borrower. China marked its accession to the Bank by investing US$350 million in IDB projects in the region, of which the largest portion, US$125 million, was earmarked for the IDB's Fund for Special Operations, which provides soft loans to Bolivia, Guyana, Haiti, Honduras, and Nicaragua.[17] The latter three countries still recognize Taiwan, not Beijing. China will hope that its IDB funding, and other fundings like it, will help to reduce the number of countries who still do not formally recognize Beijing, of which seven lie in central America and three in the Caribbean.

Latin America's proximity to the United States—and the traditional American interest in South America, as expressed in the Monroe doctrine of 1823—means that China has to walk a narrow diplomatic tightrope with respect to its Latin American involvement. Nevertheless, the years since 2000 have seen a significant extension of Chinese influence and a reduction in American influence in Latin America. In this context it is important to emphasize how dramatic the gains through trade with China have been for some of the emerging countries. Take the case of Chile, which from 1991 to 1999 ran a roughly balanced trade account with China, with total trade between the two countries not exceeding US$1.2 billion in any one year. But from 2000 Chile's exports to China, 75 percent of which are natural resources, with copper in the preponderance, started to soar. Chile's trade surplus with China increased to US$500 million in 2000, and by 2007 reached nearly US$6 billion.[18] The sharp price increases in copper and other natural resources which resulted from Chinese demand over this period not only created about two-thirds of Chile's trade surplus, but also increased very significantly the value of Chile's still unmined resources lying under the soil, greatly enhancing the value of its real estate and enterprises, and enriching its population. Between 2000 and 2007, Chile's GDP per capita more than doubled. The country's current account deficit in

2000 of US$1 billion turned into a surplus of US$7 billion in 2007. In a relatively small, lower income country such as Chile with a high dependence on natural resources and a population of 16 million, strong trade links with a large, fast-growing economy such as China completely changed the economic prospects of the country. It is easy to understand why Chile was the first Latin American country to conclude a free trade agreement with China, in 2006.

Foreign policy mistakes made by America have contributed significantly to China's success in Latin America. Recent regional polls showed that mainly negative views of the United States were held by over 50 per cent of the people in Mexico, Brazil, and Chile. The reasons for the more than 20 per cent drop in America's approval ratings were attributed by the pollsters to George W Bush's unpopularity, the attack on Iraq, and the existence of the Guantanamo detention facility. Bolivia and Venezuela both dismissed American diplomatic representation in 2008. With Cuba and Ecuador, they have moved the closest to China. Argentina, Brazil, Uruguay, and Paraguay are also now probably closer to China than they are to America, whose influence is strongest with Mexico, Chile, and the central American countries, with whom America has free trade agreements. Statements in a House Foreign Affairs Committee hearing held in Washington DC in February 2009 showed that American politicians and Latin American specialists recognize that America has lost influence in Latin America. They put this loss of influence down to neglect during the Bush years, as well as to the efforts of China and other "unfriendly" powers such as Russia and even Iran. To quote from an expert witness to the hearing, Cynthia McClintock, Professor of Political Science and International Affairs at George Washington University:

What went wrong? As elsewhere, overwhelming majorities opposed the United States war in Iraq, and the US treatment of detainees at Guantanamo. Also, the administration's welcoming of a 2002 coup against President Hugo Chavez dismayed the region's leaders. Further, we face new competition in the hemisphere. China is playing a much larger role, and the Latin American nations grew economically and have been forging their own foreign policies.[19]

The policy of the United States under George W Bush alienated all but the most loyal and dependent of America's supporters in Latin America, while the huge increase in Chinese trade since 2000, coupled with China's investment and successful efforts at developing better mutual understanding, changed the region's dynamics of diplomacy. Even though the United States remains economically the most important influence on Latin America and its number one trade partner, many Latin American countries have moved away from their traditional, quite close relationship with their powerful northern neighbor. The decision to admit China to the IDB, after years of rejection, shows how the credit crisis has weakened America's hand with respect to its Asian rival in an important region. It will be more difficult in future for the United States to resist Chinese involvement in Latin America.

China has taken advantage of the West's colonial legacy and doctrinaire approach to provide emerging countries with an attractive alternative to Western influence. The credit crisis, which has underlined China's financial strength, will reinforce China's position in the emerging world.

Endnotes

1. An expression used by Mao to describe his foreign policy after 1949.
2. Taken from Zhou Enlai's speeches.
3. "China's Influence in Africa: Implications for the United States," Peter Brookes and Ji Hye Shin, The Heritage Foundation backgrounder #1916.
4. *China Daily*, November 7, 2006.
5. The Beijing China Africa Summit of November 2006, Kenneth King, Hong Kong University.
6. *China Daily*, November 3, 2006.
7. "How China is Taking Over Africa and Why the West Should be Very Worried," Andrew Malone, *The Daily Mail*, July 18, 2008.

8. "China, Africa and Oil," Stephanie Hanson, US Council for Foreign Relations, backgrounder, June 6, 2008.

9. *China Statistical Yearbook* 2008. National Bureau of Statistics of China.

10. Ibid.

11. See http://www.cadfund.com.

12. CAD Fund prospectus. See http://www.cadfund.com.

13. "Nigeria Suspends US$9bn Contract with Beijing," Mure Dickie, *Financial Times*, November 4, 2008.

14. "On the Development of Sino–Latin American Relations," Jiang Shi Xue, Chinese Academy of Social Sciences, 2005.

15. *China Statistical Yearbook* 2008, National Bureau of Statistics of China.

16. *China Daily*, November 2004.

17. See http://www.iadb.org.

18. *China Statistical Yearbook* 2008, National Bureau of Statistics of China.

19. "US Policy Toward Latin America in 2009 and Beyond," House Foreign Affairs Committee Hearing, Washington DC, February 4, 2009.

CHAPTER

9

Nova Pax Sinica—Can China Lead the World?

C hina, a country with a huge population, much of which is poor, and with an economy still only partially developed, finds itself today holding the balance of financial power as a result of the spectacular success of its economic policies and the consequences of the financial crisis which have weakened the United States and pushed China into the global limelight. Can China rise to the challenge of global leadership, knowing that this requires it to integrate itself more thoroughly in the global political economy, expose the inner workings of its communist party system to global scrutiny, and seek assistance from other countries, particularly the United States, which it has regarded until recently as a competitor and even as an enemy? And can the rest of the world learn to live with a powerful China ruled by a communist dictatorship?

The Decline of America

Until the financial crisis of 2008, the global dominance of America and its allies seemed assured. Rooted in the post-war financial restructuring at Bretton Woods, and confirmed by the collapse of the Soviet communist system in 1990, the US dollar and the Anglo-Saxon financial system lay at the heart of the economic boom brought by globalization. Against this background of many years of American-led global growth, in September 2006 Treasury Secretary Henry Paulson traveled to Beijing to inaugurate a discussion between America and China aimed at economic cooperation. Before he left, he made a speech that recognized China's need to step onto the world stage and its reluctance to leave the shadows:

> *Some fear that China will soon overtake all other economies to the detriment of the rest of the world. To them, China has become the leading symbol of the threat posed by globalization . . . There are others—including many inside China—who argue that China is still a developing nation in transition, and that we must be patient as this transition unfolds. Both these arguments miss the greater truth. Today, China is transitioning from a planned economy to a market-driven economy and there is no doubt that this process will continue for a number of years to come. But, because of its size and its role in world markets, China is, by definition, already a global economic leader and deserves to be recognized as a leader . . . Because it is a global economic leader, what happens in China will affect the well being of the US and the rest of the world . . . As a global economic leader, China should accept its responsibility as a steward of the international system of open trade and investment. It must recognize its responsibility to maintain the health of the global system.*[1]

Were Paulson's words prophetic? Does the credit crisis mark a tipping point of historical significance, the moment when power passed from one country to another? The absence of violence makes it difficult to recognize this. For thousands of years, the passing of power could be recognized by key battles, such as Lepanto in 1571 which stopped the Turkish invasion of Europe, or Waterloo in 1815 which gave world mastery to Britain. But since the success of nuclear deterrence in the 1950s removed key battles and wars as the determinants of global leadership, financial and economic power have become the basis on which power is exercised. In 1975 America's defeat in Vietnam did not bring about a global collapse in American power. Nor did the Soviet empire vanish in 1990 because of defeat in battle. The Soviets threw in the towel because they knew that they would be bankrupted before they could match America's military might. In fact, economic resources had always helped to decide the outcome of struggles for leadership, because building and maintaining armies needed huge amounts of money. The key advantage of large countries in exercising leadership, such as France under Louis XIV in the late 1600s and early 1700s, or China a thousand years earlier under the founder of the Tang dynasty Li Yuan and his successors, was in developing and exploiting their large domestic tax bases to provide the financial resources necessary for long military campaigns.

So if economic and financial power really is the key today to global leadership, how serious is America's economic decline? Robert Reich, formerly American Labor Secretary under President Clinton and now an economics professor at the University of California, Berkley, was one of the first to publicly address the new reality. Writing in an article in London's *Financial Times* in June 2009 about the acquisition of a bankrupt General Motors by the American Government, at an effective cost of US$60 billion, he asked:

Why would US taxpayers want to own today's GM? . . . The only practical purpose I can imagine for the bail-out is to slow the decline of GM to create enough time for its workers, suppliers, dealers and communities to adjust to its eventual demise . . . US politicians dare not talk openly about industrial adjustment because the public does not want to hear about it. A strong constituency wants to preserve jobs and communities as they are, regardless of the public cost. Another equally powerful group wants to let markets work their will, regardless of the *short-term social costs. Polls show most Americans are against bailing out GM, but if their own jobs were at stake I am sure they would have a different view. So the Obama administration is, in effect, paying $60bn to buy off both constituencies. It is telling the first group that jobs and communities dependent on GM will be better preserved because of the bail-out, and the second that taxpayers and creditors will be rewarded by it. But it is not telling anyone the complete truth: GM will disappear, eventually. The bail-out is designed to give the economy time to reduce the social costs of the blow. Behind all of this is a growing public fear, of which GM's demise is a small but telling part . . . Middle-class jobs that do not need a college degree are disappearing. Job security is all but gone. And the nation is more unequal. GM in its heyday was the model of economic security and widening prosperity. Its decline has mirrored the disappearance of both. Middle-class taxpayers worry they cannot afford to bail out companies like GM. Yet they worry they cannot afford to lose their jobs . . . In many ways, what has been bad for GM has been bad for much of America.*[2]

Although China's economy still produces only a third of America's, it is projected by the IMF to contribute US$3.7 trillion or nearly a quarter of much needed world growth between 2009 and 2014—substantially more than America's expected contribution of US$2.9 trillion.[3] But, as Professor Niall Ferguson of Harvard University commented in a newspaper article on June 2, 2009, it is China's financial position that gives it the whip hand today:

Even before its economy becomes the world's biggest, China can play a much more assertive role in its relations with the United States . . . The US federal government's deficit this year will be $1.84 trillion—roughly half of total expenditure and nearly 13 per cent of GDP. Not since the Second World War has the gap between income and spending been so huge. Moreover, the Congressional Budget Office anticipates that total debt will nearly double in the decade ahead.[4]

America's power rested on its financial strength. The financial crisis, which has bankrupted the world's largest car manufacturer General

Motors and fourth largest investment bank Lehman Brothers, effectively bankrupted the world's largest insurance company AIG, and severely weakened the largest American banks, has undermined America's might. Power is passing via a means quieter, simpler, and less deadly than battle: namely, the silent transfer of funds from one account and another.

Is China Ready?

Is China qualified for leadership? In physical terms, it already is. Although projecting growth rates forward in straight lines has its dangers, and even though China's economy will take many more years to mature, it seems highly likely that China will overtake America in terms of economic size within the next two or three decades, or possibly even earlier. Only Canada has a larger landmass than China, which at 3.7 million square miles is slightly larger than the United States. At the end of 2007 its population was estimated by China itself at 1.32 billion, against a world population of 6.61 billion, making about one in five people on the planet Earth mainland Chinese. China already has a number of other "firsts" to boast of—the biggest foreign reserves, the biggest consumer of iron ore and producer of steel, the winner of the most Olympic gold medals, the biggest consumer of building materials, the biggest builder of roads and railways, and the biggest polluter in the emerging world.[5]

Moreover, the idea of China as a world leader is deeply rooted in the Chinese consciousness. Mao's place in Chinese hearts is due in part to his restoration of China's idea of itself as a country to which other countries look for guidance. But at first China shied away from attempts such as Henry Paulson's to load the responsibilities of global leadership on its shoulders, preferring to focus on its own problems and continue with the role set by Deng Xiaoping after Tiananmen Square, of keeping a low profile and hiding its strength. Since the crisis broke, however, China's pragmatic approach, forced on it by the size of the problems it faces in managing and developing a country which contains almost one-fifth of the world population, has led it to consider closer international integration, and a new role at the head of the international order.

But there are large obstacles in the way of China assuming the leadership role that Paulson and Geithner would have it play. One is economic. Geithner's June 2009 speech in Beijing cast America and China as global partners, who would rise and fall together, and placed a high degree of dependence for economic recovery and rebalancing on the ability of both countries to adjust their patterns of economic demand: America's towards more saving, and China's towards less saving and more spending.[6] But while an increase in America's savings rate, whether government-decreed or not, is already happening by force of circumstance, China's economic structure may only change slowly in the next few years. The relative immaturity of its economy will preclude it from pulling the world towards economic recovery as fast and as powerfully as many in the developed world would like. In the absence of the deep, disruptive structural reform of the kind carried out by Zhu Rongji between 1995 and 2000 which gave the Chinese economy its current shape, China has a limited capacity to make the economic adjustments that are deemed necessary to fully rebalance global demand and bring about sustained global recovery.

Zhu Rongji's main task, as he saw it, was not to dismantle the State-owned sector in favor of private free enterprise, but to enhance it by making it work better. In this he largely succeeded. The result is that all the key sectors in the Chinese economy, such as energy, banking and other financial services, logistics, communications, construction, and even retail are dominated by very large, highly profitable enterprises owned and controlled by the Chinese State. The great economic hardship in the middle and late 1990s that China suffered as a result of these reforms is widely unrecognized. The government's termination of the social obligations of those monopolistic State enterprises which were not closed but restructured, removed enormous cost and produced large windfall profits. Meanwhile, many millions of underage retirees were forced to eke out their remaining days as the guests of their next-of-kin, who obey their Confucian traditions, if not their own inclinations, by providing their parents and close relatives with shelter and food. Today, China's economic success has changed the Chinese mood. Another huge sacrifice on anything like the scale of 15 years ago would not find acceptance among the Chinese people. Incremental structural adjustment is probably the best path—in terms of reform—that can be hoped for in China today.

Careful examination of the facts raises questions as to how the desired switch in Chinese economic growth, towards private or household spending as a principal driver, can occur within the time span of a few years which is demanded by developed countries. The main force behind China's economy since the late 1990s has been the reinvestment, via government allocation and the State-owned banking system, of the large profits from State-owned companies into capital goods and infrastructure. This spending, more than the export sector or private consumption, has driven Chinese growth since Zhu Rongji's reforms, and will continue to do so in the near term. The importance of investment in Chinese growth is obvious both from China's own statistics and from the dramatic increases in the world prices of oil and every other kind of commodity and building material since 2000. The expansion of Chinese household spending at anything like the same rate as investment has been limited by the high Chinese savings rate and by the very modest means of most of China's households, so that the relative contribution to China's fast economic growth from this source has diminished. In 2007, China's huge rural population, which accounts for about two-thirds of the Chinese population, produced only one-quarter of total household spending, and food made up 40 percent of the rural Chinese household budget.[7] As they become richer, people spend less on basic necessities, but in China's countryside, survival is still at the top of most families' agendas. One reason for this is that, after an early period of fast rural development after 1978, China's Government from 1990 focused on the towns, with the result that the incomes of China's urban residents caught up and then overtook those of the farmers in the countryside. The introduction of mortgages on town real estate in the late 1990s—together with the right to buy, sell, and rent property—has enriched many Chinese town dwellers. But until very recently, Chinese farmers have had no rights over their land. In fact, it has been estimated that over 60 million Chinese rural dwellers have had their land taken from them by local officials with nominal compensation and sold on for development at a high price. However, the regime led by Hu Jintao and Wen Jiabao, which came to power in 2002, has been much more conscious of the rural areas. In October 2008, a new Chinese Communist Party resolution focusing on the importance of the countryside stated that farmland could be bought, sold, or rented, giving Chinese farmers the same right as urban residents to monetize their principal asset.[8] Although it is still too early to be sure, this reform could transform the spending power of the Chinese countryside. But even with this new development, it is not likely that Chinese private spending can provide any meaningful support to the world economy in the short or medium term. In 2007, the most recent year for which reliable records of the Chinese economy are available at the time of writing, the amount of Chinese investment exceeded the amount of Chinese household spending by 1.5 times.[9] China's domestic demand will probably continue to be driven by investment for the next few years. The economic assistance that Chinese growth can provide to the rest of the world over this time scale will be focused largely on countries that are rich in natural resources, who can feed China's appetite for construction.

The emphasis on investment spending to drive China's growth was reinforced by China's announcement, in November 2008, of a very large program of spending to offset the effects of the collapse in developed country economies. The announcement sparked local governments in China into immediately starting to plan for what they saw as a one-off, golden opportunity to get their favorite projects approved as part of the central government's spending announcement.[10] The head of a county in Shanxi province is quoted as urging his colleagues at a specially convened meeting less than a week after the November announcement to:

. . . take advantage of an extremely rare and precious opportunity . . . we must concentrate our forces, and act quickly, strengthen our links with the provincial and municipal authorities, and make sure that more keypoint investment projects come to our county . . . Getting more project funding is our top current task.[11]

The analysis shows that half the funds allocated to the stimulus plan (revised amount 3 trillion yuan or US$440 billion equivalent) are earmarked for spending on roads, railways, airports, and the electricity grid. Most of the rest will go to other kinds of public works, such as affordable housing and village infrastructure. While this huge financial stimulus, amounting in total to around 13 percent of China's GDP, will reinforce China's growth over the next few years, it will shift the main driver of China's economy even further towards the State sector and government spending, away from private consumption.

The American economy badly needs other countries to buy American exports and invest their savings in America to support its financial system. In the Japanese and German experiences, big revaluations of the Japanese yen and German mark against the dollar did not succeed in correcting the large Japanese and German trade surpluses. This shows that a change in savings habits would probably be much more important in correcting the imbalances between America and China than a permanent revaluation of the Chinese yuan against the US dollar and the euro. But it does look as if China, at least in its household sector, could maintain a high savings rate, while starting to draw down savings balances to support an increasingly large retired population: the opposite of what the Americans need it to do. A high Chinese household savings rate will not help to reduce the large surplus in China's external trade account or the American deficit with China. China's external surpluses may reduce only slowly. Continuing Chinese large surpluses would not have good consequences for China's relationship with America. But if the Chinese Government was doing all it reasonably could to stimulate domestic growth short of destabilizing its own economy and increasing unemployment, what could America do, given that it will be dependent on foreign buyers of its debt for years to come, of which China will be one of the most important? Developed countries must be patient and allow China's economy to mature before private consumption can start to take over from investment as the most important growth driver. But Americans are not a people noted for their patience, and the increase in Chinese global influence may not always be a smooth process.

Another big hurdle for China to surmount in exerting its new-found global power is in adjusting to the very different expectations that other, particularly non-Asian, countries have of their leaders. For China to command more than the grudging respect of the peoples of other countries, it has to inspire as well as impress. America, the other superpower, has led not just by dint of its financial strength, but by setting an example of freedom and choice based on the right of the individual—a shining moral standard, whose tarnishing by the attacks on Afghanistan and Iraq and the operation of the prison at Guantanamo Bay only serves to highlight the importance of this aspect to America's leadership. China, on the other hand, is governed by the 77-million strong communist party which is rigidly controlled from the top, still using self-criticism and thought sessions in which the sayings and writings of previous leaders Mao Zedong, Deng Xiaoping, and Jiang Zemin are analyzed and studied, along with the contribution of current leader Hu Jintao's "scientific development concept" as "the latest achievement in adapting Marxism to Chinese characteristics."[12] China's attempt in 2008 to take overseas its mission for acceptance via the Olympic torch parade met with embarrassing rejection in France, America, and other developed countries. How can people around the world come to relate the Chinese State and its values to their search for freedom and self-respect? The Chinese answer—that a full belly and a roof over one's head are more important than democracy and human rights—cannot satisfy human yearnings. East Asian countries can understand and respect Confucian values which manifest themselves in systems governed by authoritarian figures. To them, the Chinese system is something they can respect, if not admire. But to the developed West, the question of Chinese democracy will always remain—when and how? As the distinguished Russian sinologist and diplomat Sergey Tikhvinsky notes:

Markets are not a substitute for ethics, religion, and civilization. Markets have never set aims to achieve beauty, or equity, sustainability and spirituality. The market's goals are far from a common human mission.[13]

An imaginative answer to this is that a Taiwan united with the Chinese mainland could bring the young, Chinese democratic tradition of the Kuomintang from Taipei to Beijing, supported by a United States which is presently divided in its loyalties between the two contenders for the rights to the Chinese mainland. Certainly Sun Yat-Sen's significance as the founder of the modern Chinese State, if not Chinese democracy, is something both the Taiwanese and the mainland can agree on. But it is probably fanciful to consider the possibility, for a generation at least, of any kind of democracy in mainland China which a Western country could recognize. There are no signs presently of the Chinese Communist Party giving up its grip. In fact, China's economic success and the swiftness and effectiveness of the leadership's recent response to the economic crisis which spread from the West in late 2008 have reinforced the status quo.

The survival of the Communist Party in China could be given a more sinister appearance by the wave of Chinese nationalism which has emerged as China has become more powerful. The first signs of this trend appeared in the mid-1990s, when a book appeared in China called *China Can Say No; Political and Emotional Choices in the Post-Cold War Era*. With chapters entitled "We Don't Want MFN" (trade benefits accorded by the US, known as Most Favored Nation status), and "I Won't Get on a Boeing 777," the authors struck out against US foreign policy—particularly where it involved support for Taiwan over mainland China—and American individualism, claimed that China was being used as a scapegoat for American problems, and voiced support for countries whose governments openly declared their opposition to America, such as Cuba.[14] The book accused Japan of being a client state of the United States, opposed Japan's bid for a seat on the UN Security Council and supported a renewed call for war reparations to China from Japan. *China Can Say No* became a bestseller and set off a vehement and emotional popular nationalism often critical of the Chinese Government for not standing up firmly enough for China's dignity.

The Chinese Government learned quickly how to harness Chinese nationalism as a force in support of its foreign policy objectives. The violent demonstrations in Beijing in May 1999 following NATO's bombing of the Chinese consulate in Belgrade were encouraged and orchestrated by the Chinese Government, who arranged buses to bring Chinese students in from different university campuses to throw stones and shout slogans at the American embassy. In September 2004, protests appeared online directed against an advertisement of Nippon Paint in Guangdong, a southern Chinese province, which depicted a traditional Chinese pavilion with carved dragons coiled up around its front pillars. One of the dragons was pictured slumped at the bottom of a pillar painted a shinier red than all the others. The advertisement's message was that Nippon's lacquer, used to coat that pillar, was so smooth that even the dragon, a symbol of Chinese sovereignty and strength, slid down it. *People's Daily Online* published an article entitled "How Can We Recognise International Advertising That Harms National Dignity?" The article raised the question whether the advertiser's defense—that it wished merely to educate readers and invite discussion about negative trends in advertising—should be accepted as a genuine apology or seen as an effort to raise sales through deliberate provocation. All the responses selected were negative, with the most outspoken calling for a boycott of Nippon Paint.[15] In 2005, the refusal of the Japanese Premier to tone down his annual visit to the shrine of Japan's war dead resulted in demonstrations against Japan organized by the Chinese Government in several Chinese cities.

Not everyone in China has strong nationalist feelings. In a Chinese survey of nearly 52,000 people, 41 percent agreed with the statement that the Nippon Paint advertisement "was a provocation to our national feelings." But the other 59 percent took a more moderate view; 23 percent thought that it was "good, but failed to take into account national sentiment," and 19 percent thought that it was "a good, creative advertisement." The results of a 2006 survey (carried out according to Chinese regulations in partnership with a local organization, and vetted by the government before the release of results) suggest that attitudes towards Japan are not universally negative. While 70 percent of those polled held "unfavorable" views towards Japan, 21 percent had "favorable" views, and in the case of the United States, those with favorable views (47 percent) outnumbered the unfavorable ones (43 percent).[16]

China and Overseas Investment

But while Chinese nationalism will remain a powerful undercurrent, popular sentiment within China will encourage foreign engagement. After all, China will continue to have its own strong self-interest in building warm and cooperative relationships with developed countries. Exports may not grow at the average annual rate of 24 percent that they did between 2000 and 2008, but they will continue to be very important to China. Outward investment will become even more important. China has a strong need to recycle some of its enormous trade and capital surpluses into overseas assets which can provide China with the resources and knowhow it needs for its development, as well as a stream of dividend income. In 2009 China took some important steps in the direction of encouraging overseas investment, bringing the approvals process down in March from the central government to provincial or municipal level for investments of US$100 million or less, and releasing in April its first guidelines for overseas investment by Chinese companies. In the non-financial sector Chinese outbound investment rose by 63.5 percent in 2008 to US$41 billion.[17] China would like to see this figure expand significantly. But China is not perceived as a "friendly" investor by many countries, and faces major hurdles when it comes to buying controlling or even minority stakes in assets considered strategic by their host countries.

So far China's drive to increase outward investment into developed countries has met with more failure than success. In June 2009, China's national aluminum holding company Chinalco abandoned its US$19.5 billion bid to increase its minority stake in one of the world's largest resources companies Rio Tinto to nearly 20 percent. Opposition in Australia to Chinese ownership of Australian-based mines was expressed through advertisements aired on Australian television accusing Kevin Rudd, the Australian Prime Minister, of bearing gifts to the Chinese military regime by allowing control of strategic mineral resources in Australia.

While Rio tried to persuade its shareholders to go ahead, a recovery in Rio's share price undercut on both sides the economic rationale for the transaction. If it had gone ahead, the acquisition would have given Chinalco a direct interest in some of Rio's richest mines in Australia, Chile, and America in aluminum, copper, and iron ore, as well as a preferred status in buying iron ore, copper, and other resources from Rio at good prices and in sufficient volumes. A similar hands-off signal was sent to China in 2005 when furious opposition forced the American Government to reject a Chinese acquisition of the significant American oil company Unocal in 2005. In the same year, State-controlled Chinese computer manufacturer Lenovo had to divest IBM's American Government consulting and procurement business before acquiring IBM.

At the same time, China was one of the first stops when the Western banking industry needed fast cash after markets nosedived at the beginning of the financial crisis in late 2007 and in early 2008. As a result Chinese State-owned entities hold substantial minority stakes in a few major Western-based financial services companies, including American investment bank Morgan Stanley, British bank Barclays, and private equity fund manager Blackstone. The country's state wealth fund established a joint US$4 billion fund with specialist financial sector private equity investor JC Flowers in early 2008, and China added a further US$1 billion to its Morgan Stanley investment in June 2009. But while China has been able to become a shareholder in some important foreign financial services companies, the sectors it would most like to enter through overseas investment—namely high technology and natural resources, which both offer very important strategic benefits—are apparently out of bounds. The failure of the Chinalco investment shows that China's rising international profile and the success of the Beijing Olympics has not significantly changed public perception of its hostile potential in countries such as Australia, where it would like to have a large ownership footprint. Yet the strategic requirement for China to invest overseas will not go away, but rather increase. China therefore needs to work out new ways to persuade other countries of its friendly and peaceful intentions. Rather like a "nouveau riche" who has just entered society and needs an experienced society hand to help him avoid making social gaffes and introduce him around,

China needs a helping hand from global club insiders such as America to help it settle down in its new role of overseas investor, banker to the developed world, and global leader.

Although there are obvious barriers to China's emerging global power and influence, the country's own need to develop and its deeply felt right to world leadership, plus the strong interest that America and its other major partners have in promoting its success and development, China will probably overcome them. The likeliest scenario is that increased mutual understanding between China and America will develop a successful partnership between the two superpowers, of the kind envisaged by Henry Paulson when he was American Treasury Secretary. China will strongly resist the development of a global top table with only two seats at it, however, and will look for broader mechanisms than a G2 for developing its global influence. In this context, the envelopment of Taiwan by mainland China, which the interdependence and relative sizes of the two countries appears to make an inevitability, will remove one of the key sources of tension between China and the United States, thereby greatly assisting China's global integration and encouraging the Chinese system to open up more to liberal influences.

However, one should not entirely discount another scenario, under which a series of misunderstandings and unfortunate events cause China to fall out with America and its allies, and turn instead towards Russia and China's friends in Africa and Latin America to form an anti-West coalition. How could this happen? Sustained American support for an increasingly independent Taiwan, a sudden rise in tension in the South China Sea around Chinese and Japanese rival claims, or uncompromising Chinese actions in Tibet and on the Sino–Indian border, which threatened the Dalai Lama and provoked strong reactions in the United States could all be triggers for a falling out. It might be argued that no American president would be short-sighted or foolish enough to entertain a pro-Taiwanese, anti-Chinese policy, but a similarly hopeful prediction made 10 years ago about the undertaking of further dangerous adventures in the Middle East would have been proved wrong, and so one cannot entirely discount such a development, in spite of the closeness of the economic ties that now exist between China and the

West. The division of the world once again into two armed camps, each led by a superpower, would cut global growth, lead to local fights over resources, and probably bring much worse. The peaceful route forward is much more likely simply because it serves everyone's interests, particularly China's, much better.

Now that America's financial weakness has handicapped it, the Chinese Government feels that showing leadership is the best way to advance its agenda. China's goal is not world domination or to go to war with America, but to develop China to its full extent. This is a task that will fully occupy it for the next 100 years and more, and will increasingly engage it with the rest of the world. In turn the world will occupy itself more and more with China.

Endnotes

1. Remarks by Henry Paulson on the International Economy, September 13, 2006, US–China Strategic Economic Dialogue, US Treasury Web site.
2. "General Motors Holds a Mirror up to America," Robert Reich, *Financial Times*, May 31, 2009.
3. IMF projections. See http://www.imf.org.
4. "The Trillion Dollar Question—China or America?" Niall Ferguson, *Daily Telegraph*, June 2, 2009.
5. Estimates are from the World Bank. http://www.worldbank.org.
6. Speech by Secretary Tim Geithner, "The United States and China, Cooperating for Recovery and Growth," Peking University, Beijing, June 1, 2009.
7. *China Statistical Yearbook* 2008, National Bureau of Statistics of China.
8. "Hu Jintao's Land Reform," Cheng Li, *China Leadership Monitor*, no. 27, Hoover Institution, Stanford University.
9. *China Statistical Yearbook* 2008, National Bureau of Statistics of China.
10. "Understanding the Chinese Stimulus Package," Barry Naughton, *China Leadership Monitor*, no. 28, Hoover Institution, Stanford University.
11. Ibid.
12. "The Political Implications of China's Growing Middle Class," Joseph Fewsmith, *China Leadership Monitor*, no. 21, Hoover Institution.

13. From *The Vital Triangle*, Alterman & Garver.
14. See blogs at http://www.danwei.org.
15. *People's Daily*, September 2004.
16. *People's Daily*, September 2006.
17. *People's Daily*, January 2009.

10

New China, Old China

Talking at the beginning of 2009 to several of my colleagues on the teaching staff of the Guanghua business school at Peking University, I was struck by their disdainful attitude towards the West, and particularly the United States. "America has brought us a lot of trouble," they said. "We don't want to import America's problems into China. We shouldn't imitate their system. We should look for our future here, not there." Has the credit crisis punctured the bubble of Western superiority in China which gained ground from the early 1990s, as China struggled to adopt capitalist ideas and methods?

Since the death of Mao in 1976, and the end of the Cultural Revolution a few months later which signaled the beginning of China's return to normality, one can describe three general stages through which Chinese society has passed. The first stage is called in China "healing the wounds." On my arrival in China in the late 1980s it was not the poverty and mass of blue tunics that got my attention, it was the dull vacant gaze and the look of hopelessness in the faces of many late middle-aged and elderly Chinese that I met or passed in the street. Years of uncertainty and arbitrary brutality in the 1960s and 1970s left their mark on the lives of many middle-aged and older Chinese, who lacked the energy to forget, recover, and start again. After the promising green shoots of growth that appeared in the 1980s, the clamp-down which followed the brutal student suppression of June 1989 in Tiananmen Square seemed to confirm the hopelessness of China's situation. Until the mid- to late 1990s, the dullness and sadness of Chinese writing, painting, and poetry still reflected society's shock and its attempt to come to terms with its immediate past.

But around the mid-1990s, China stopped feeling sorry for itself and started living again. This was marked by the return of young Chinese who had gone overseas to be educated at the West's glittering universities, and to work for leading Western law firms, banks, consulting companies, and multinationals. Some returnees to China were originally from Taiwan and arrived in China via America, others came from Chinese families who had settled years before in North America, and yet others were Chinese sent overseas on government scholarships to study in the 1980s and early 1990s, who saw opportunity in basing their careers back in China. Some of the most important positions in Chinese Government, business, and academia today are now occupied by graduates from Western universities. Yi Gang, today a Deputy Governor of China's central bank the People's Bank of China, gained his doctorate in economics in America, and was awarded tenure as a professor at Indiana University before returning in 1994 as a research fellow and economics teacher at Peking University. Gao Xiqing, now president of China's influential wealth fund the China Investment Corporation, returned to China with a JD in law from America's Duke University in 1986, to become one of the first directors of China's securities regulator, the China Securities Regulatory Commission in 1992. Zhang Wei Ying, the dean of Peking University's Guanghua School of Management and one of China's most influential and radical economists, studied at Oxford University until 1994 for his doctorate in economics under Nobel Prize winner Sir James Mirrlees. Other returnees focused on making money, either as highly paid consultants and investment bankers employed by prestigious Western institutions such as McKinsey, Booz Allen, and Morgan Stanley, or as entrepreneurs. China's new companies, such as dot-coms Sina and Sohu which listed in New York in the late 1990s, were led by Chinese nationals who had studied at top graduate schools in America. The Chinese President's son-in-law Daniel Mao, chief executive of Sina at the time it listed on the NASDAQ in 1999, went to Stanford University in California, after graduating from Shanghai's Jiaotong University.

This wave of talented, high-profile Chinese achievers returned to China wearing Western clothes, drinking Starbucks coffee, and with Western ideas in their heads, but also with a deeply felt respect and love for Chinese history and culture. Their success and charisma advertised Western values to the Chinese, at the same time as companies such as Coca-Cola, Procter and Gamble, Unilever, Carrefour, and Mercedes-Benz were bringing Western advertising and Western consumerism to China. Western values became cool. Chinese people who had earlier described Coca-Cola as tasting like cough syrup, and had turned up their noses at the thought of drinking milk and eating cheese, started to buy Western cars, washing machines, and dishwashers, took up golf and tennis, took out mortgages, and read the Chinese edition of *Fortune*.

The influx of Western values into China coincided with the beginnings of a Chinese middle class. Research done in China in 1995–96 found little evidence of a middle class, but the same researcher five years later found that the number of Chinese people with a sense of class awareness had increased dramatically.[1] The Chinese perception of middle class is based not just on money but on a college education and a white-collar job. Using these criteria, studies done between 2000 and 2002 put the size of the Chinese middle class at no larger than 50 million people, or about 6 percent of the population—small, but increasing rapidly. Many more Chinese described themselves as middle class than actually were; 46 percent of the respondents in one survey and 85 percent of those in another described themselves as middle class, indicating perhaps that large parts of Chinese society now subscribe to middle-class property-owning and consumption values. Chinese people appear not to dislike the idea of inequality in itself, but to resent it when it arises from the exercise of power or status, and not from success in a competitive environment. The desire for political participation is stronger within the middle class, both in government and in the private sector, than lower down, but is still weak. When asked in one survey to rank a number of activities—including developing one's own career, consumption, leisure, political participation, and family life—most respondents ranked political participation last.

Although China's aping of Western ideas and lifestyles brought a negative reaction from some young Chinese students and professionals who expressed their disgust online and in art and literature, most of China's new middle class identified with Western values. Many Chinese believed that the West was better than China, not because it was more democratic, but because it was richer and could offer its people a better lifestyle. It was widely believed that to develop itself further, China had to become more like the United States.

But then came the financial crisis, the collapse of some of the West's fabled icons, and the realization in China that, post-crisis, Chinese banks were stronger and larger than the American or European ones, that the Chinese yuan might be a better store of value than the once-mighty US dollar, and that the West depended as much, if not more, on China than the other way around. The idea in China of Western superiority has been undermined by the crisis. Its place has been taken by the memory that China was the largest and richest country in the world for a period more than twice as long as the whole of America's documented history. A sophisticated and meritocratic Chinese governing class organized and controlled a country which, at its economic height in the early 1700s, accounted for around one-third of the world's population and economic output. Is not a society superior to any other that in the second century BC invented paper and ball bearings, used natural gas as fuel, and understood how blood circulated around the body?[2] The immortal words of China's most famous poet remind us of the early sophistication of Chinese society:[3]

Thoughts in the Silent Night

Beside my bed, a pool of light
Is it hoarfrost on the ground?
I lift my head and see the moon
I look down, and think of home

Li Bai (701–762)

At the height of its civilization, between 1,100 and 1,500 years ago, outsiders and foreigners could only acknowledge China's strength and cultural superiority. Any other response to China was not based on reality or common sense. Over many centuries, the Chinese feeling of superiority became innate, something so ingrained that Chinese people were hardly aware of it. It has been reawoken by the credit crisis. From China's ancient dominance, today's Chinese draw their innate sense of superiority and sophistication. From its nineteenth-century demise at foreign hands, they draw their determination never again to be humiliated. From the reunification of China under the communists they draw their independence and spirit.

People in China saw the financial crisis quite differently from other countries. At the end of March 2009, a large survey was conducted in China, Japan, South Korea, the United States, Britain, France, and Germany to measure attitudes to the global economic crisis. The survey showed a much higher popular indifference to the economic crisis in China than in other Asian or G8 countries. Chinese public opinion views the economic crisis in the West with a sense of detachment similar to that which colored the view taken by Americans and Europeans of the Asian economic crisis and the Russian debt default in 1997 and 1998. In China the proportion of respondents who thought the crisis would not affect their economy much was 35 percent, compared with an average of eight percent of respondents over the six non-Chinese countries that were surveyed. The number of people in China who thought the downturn would last more than two years was 13 percent; in the other countries sampled, the average number was 36 percent. And 55 percent of Japanese and 83 percent of South Koreans but only 20 percent of Chinese thought that this was a bad time to spend.[4]

The credit crisis has ended the Chinese love affair with the West, and focused attention back on China. In 1999, half of my MBA class at Peking University were Chinese who wanted to work for foreign companies in Beijing and Shanghai. In 2009, half were Europeans, Koreans, Americans, and Canadians who wanted to learn Chinese and work in China. The Chinese middle class still play golf, but now they watch dramas on Chinese Central Television about Chinese history and Chinese policemen, buy a luxury car made in Shanghai, and listen to Chinese pop music. And they are turning to Chinese ideas and values for inspiration in their business and personal lives. The research of Henri-Claude de Bettignies of the China European Business School in Shanghai and Nandani Lynton of Thunderbird Business school in America shows that young Chinese businesspeople and entrepreneurs, an important group of opinion influencers in China, are turning away from Western values and searching for moral roots in China. Their article "Seeking Moral Leadership in China" comments:

> *Chinese professionals in Shanghai and Beijing are concerned about the financial disaster that has spread from New York and London throughout the world. They read the Western press that blames both individual executive greed and false belief in the inherent self-control of the capitalist market system; they worry about their own real estate values dropping; they question Adam Smith's notion of the invisible hand of the market as Western governments nationalize private banks. And they shake their heads. The West has lost any moral high ground it has had, and some now are wondering whether China can save the world from collapse.*[5]

They note that a recent book by Yu Dan commenting on Confucian thought topped the non-fiction bestseller lists in China for months, and quote the example of a 45-year-old Shanghai MBA from a top-ranked Western business school, with experience working with successful entrepreneurs and the founder of his own investment firm, who has over the last three years become so deeply Buddhist that he rises to meditate at 5 a.m. daily, eats little, works hard but gives away much of his income. "What do I actually need?" he asks. "Very little for myself." An older executive running a midsized company opens a business presentation with a slide on Taoism and states that China seems to have a religion of money but in fact must learn to rely on the Doctrine of the Mean or the balance exemplified by the symbol of the Yin and Yang.[6]

While the self-denying idealism of the young Chinese professionals quoted above may not be the rule, China's relative immunity to the financial destruction wrought by the tsunami from New York has convinced many Chinese that the West doesn't have all the answers, and China will be safer and can do better if it follows its own instincts. In fact, the Chinese have always treated advice given them by outsiders, such as foreign governments and advisors, with care, insisting on the uniqueness of China's own situation, and even on occasion ignoring external views and prescriptions. Now the apparent financial and moral weakness of the West serves to confirm China's belief that the solution to its economic and spiritual development needs can be found within China's own history and philosophy. Chinese thought and behavior is still strongly influenced by Confucian order and obedience, as well as by Taoist unity with nature. Neither of these two ancient strands of Chinese philosophy can easily marry with Western ideals which support the idea of freedom, in individual thought and behavior, as well as in financial markets. If Chinese object to the way that they are governed, it is not because they dislike living in a police state—after all, as they will tell you, one is as likely to feel spied on via close-circuit television in London as in Shanghai, and there are as many policemen on display in New York as there are in Beijing—but because they hate the corruption that a one-party political system inevitably brings. In choosing whether to live in California or Shanghai, a Chinese person will consider the ease with which he or she can make and keep money, eat Chinese food, visit relatives, and even the weather before worrying about being able to exercise a choice at the ballot box. Stability, strength, and everyday competence are the key factors that these people look for in their government. Most Chinese people feel that the credit crisis has confirmed the Chinese system, even with its disadvantages, as more stable, and therefore more dependable and desirable, than the Western system. By apparently undermining the viability of the Western economic system, the crisis has removed the only possible contender to the Chinese system, and made any serious challenge to the Chinese Communist Party's rule even more unlikely in the foreseeable future.

However, in the longer term a major political challenge does exist for China. The huge economic problem remains of bringing material comforts which are considered standard in the West to most of its huge rural population. This could take many more years to achieve. But in the economic size league, success in overtaking Britain, France, Germany, and soon Japan leaves only the United States ahead of China. The Chinese communist system is starting to outgrow the vision of its founding fathers Mao and Deng. Successive Chinese leaders have focused on getting from A to B, where B represents outgrowing the United States. Then what? As a result of promotions made to China's inner governing circle, the Standing Committee of the Politburo, in late 2007, we now know who the next leaders of China will be when the guard next changes in 2012. Hu Jintao will probably be succeeded by a well-connected princeling, Xi Jinping, and Wen Jiabao by Li Keqiang, an Anhui-born Peking University law graduate and protégé of Hu Jintao. Both have arrived at their high positions after many years of careful endeavor. Neither is likely to bring major change to China. And as China continues to grow, it gets nearer to reaching the goal set by former leader Deng, of being world number one. What should its purpose be once this point has been reached? Chinese Premier Wen Jiabao addressed this point in a revealing answer he made to the editor of the *Financial Times* in an interview:

> **Lionel Barber:** Looking to the future, could you imagine there being direct elections to the National Peoples Congress in, say, 10 years' time?
>
> **Wen Jiabao:** Well, actually, I think economic life and political life are not separable from each other. Let me address this political question from you from an economic perspective. We are undertaking both economic restructuring and political restructuring, and both are very important. Without the successful political restructuring, one can't ensure success in our economic restructuring. The goal in our political restructuring is to promote socialist democracy, and better ensure people's rights to democratic election, democratic decision making, democratic management, and

democratic supervision. The society that we desire is one of equity and justice, is one in which people can achieve all round development in a free and equal environment. That is also why I like Adam Smith's *Theory of Moral Sentiments* very much . . . Adam Smith made excellent arguments . . . he said in the book that if fruits of a society's economic development cannot be shared by all, it is morally unsound and risky, as it is bound to jeopardize social stability. If the wealth of a society is concentrated in the hands of a small number of people then this is against the popular will, and the society is bound to be unstable. Like truth is the primary virtue in thinking, I have always believed that justice and equity are the primary virtues in the socialist system. In the eyes of the West, it seems that the Chinese are afraid of democracy or elections. Actually, this is not true . . . Now we have direct elections at village level and also direct elections of People's Deputies at Township level . . . I have always believed that if the people have the ability to run the village affairs well they are capable of running the town affairs well and the county affairs and then the provincial affairs. In this entire process we should take a step by step approach in the light of China's own conditions and to develop a democracy with Chinese features.[7]

In fact, since Hu Jintao's accession to power in 2003, he has not encouraged more liberalism within the Communist Party, as he was widely expected to do, but used a tighter control of the party to reverse the modest moves towards a more liberal and open Chinese society that occurred under his predecessor Jiang Zemin. At the same time, there are also signs that China is becoming more of a rule-based society which depends less on the arbitrary whims of one person. While President Hu Jintao has consolidated his power over the various factions within the Chinese Communist Party, the strongest of which had been the so-called Shanghai gang led by previous President Jiang Zemin, decisions seem to be taken on a consensual basis. For example, it is believed that Hu Jintao tried hard to get his protégé Li Keqiang nominated to succeed him as President, rather than Wen Jiabao as Prime Minister, but was unable to obtain support to do this. Hu Jintao's regime has not been marked by any weakening in the Communist Party's grip on China: quite the reverse. But he has used traditional party procedures to encourage an embracing by the ruling communist party of Jiang Zemin's idea of a mixed capitalist and socialist economy, in place of Marxist-Leninism and the triumph of the workers, and his own contribution of Harmonious Society and Peaceful Development, together with scientific technological thought which can bring the Communist Party up to date. In fact Wen Jiabao's expression, in his interview with the *Financial Times*, of a society with equity and justice, "one in which people can achieve all round development in a free and equal environment" is a translation of Hu's theory of Harmonious Development. It might seem to a Western observer, brought up on Rousseau, the rights of man, and the Fifth Amendment, that the Chinese would at some point have to rebel against a one-party dictatorship based on a discredited communist ideology. But there are few signs of suppressed desire for a multi-party system in China. Instead the indications are that many Chinese would simply like the present system to work better, with less corruption and abuse of power by insiders. China's political system does not appear to be threatened, in spite of the fact that some Westerners feel that it should be. This is probably because most Chinese see it as operating adequately and meeting China's development needs. If China's one-party system can follow Darwin's dictum, that the species which survive are not the biggest or the strongest but those who can adapt to change, then it can probably continue for many years to come. The likely prospect that we face is of a one-party Chinese system that attempts to become more acceptable to the rest of the world by demonstrating its ability to manage China's ascendancy peacefully. After all, although other Asian nations nominally have multi-party rule, many of them operate "de facto" one-party systems. It would be a mistake for Westerners to assume that China's system is doomed because it is different to their own.

Endnotes

1. "The Political Implications of China's Growing Middle Class," Joseph Fewsmith, *China Leadership Monitor*, no. 21, Hoover Institution.
2. *Science and Civilisation in China*, Joseph Needham, Cambridge University Press, 2004.
3. *A Selection of Classical Chinese Poems*, Chinese Esperanto Press, People's Republic of China, 1996.
4. N-Dynamic Market Research & Consultancy, *China Daily*, April 2009.
5. "Seeking Moral Leadership in China," Nandani Lynton & Henri-Claude de Bettignies, China European International Business School, Shanghai, 2009.
6. Ibid.
7. Transcript of Interview with Wen Jiabao, *Financial Times*, February 2, 2009.

Bibliography

A Selection of Chinese Classical Poems with Illustrations, People's Republic of China: China Esperanto Press, 1996.

Adams, James et al. "China: From Poor Areas to Poor People: China's Evolving Poverty Reduction Agenda." World Bank, March 2009.

Alterman, Jon B, and John Garvey. *The Vital Triangle: China, the United States and the Middle East*. Washington DC: Centre for Strategic and International Studies, 2008.

Altman, Roger. "A Weakening of the West." *Foreign Affairs*, January/February 2009.

Andrews, Edmund. "Greenspan's Speech Focuses on Deflation, not Inflation." *New York Times*, December 20, 2002.

BP Statistical Review of World Energy, June 2009.

Bank of England, Lending Data 1998–2008.

Bank of England, *Quarterly Bulletin*, 2007.

Bauer, P T. *Equality, the Third World and Economic Delusion*. London: Weidenfeld & Nicolson, 1981.

Bean, Charles. "Globalisation and Inflation." Bank of England. Speech to the London School of Economics, October 24, 2006.

Becker, Jasper. *Dragon Rising: An Inside Look at China Today*. London: Random House, 2007.

Bernanke, Ben. "Deflation: Making Sure 'It' Doesn't Happen Here." Speech to National Economists Club, Washington DC. November 21, 2002.

Bernanke, Ben. "Global Imbalances—Recent Developments and Prospects." Bundesbank Lecture, Berlin. September 11, 2007.

Bernanke, Ben. "The Global Savings Glut and the US Current Account Deficit." Sandridge Lecture, Virginia Association of Economics. March 10, 2005.

Bernanke, Ben, and Mark Gertler. "Monetary Policy and Asset Price Volatility." Bank of Kansas City, *Economic Review*, Fourth Quarter 1999.

Bernanke, Ben, and Mark Gertler. "Should Central Banks Respond to Movements in Asset Prices?" *The American Economic Review*, vol. 91, no. 2, Papers and Proceedings of the Hundred Thirteenth Annual Meeting of the American Economic Association (May 2001), pp 253–257.

Bernanke, Ben, Vincent Reinhart, and Sack Brian. "Monetary Policy Alternatives at the Zero Bound—An Empirical Assessment." Federal Reserve Bank System, 2004.

Bonavia, David. *The Chinese*. London: Allen Lane, 1981.

Broadman, Harry G. "Africa's Silk Road; China and India's New Economic Frontier." World Bank, 2007.

Brown, Lester. "Plan B 3.0 Mobilizing to Save Civilisation." Earth Policy Institute, 2008.

Buckles, Aron, Lt Cmdr, United States Navy. "The United States Navy and PLA Navy: Linchpin of the US Military Strategy Towards the People's Republic of China." Masters Thesis, US Marine Corps, Quantico, Virginia, 2006.

Butterfield, Fox. *China Alive in the Bitter Sea*. London: Hodder & Stoughton, 1982.

Byrd, William et al. "China's Rural Industry." Edited by World Bank, 1990.

"Central Asian Perceptions of China." Special issue of *The China and Eurasia Forum Quarterly*, vol. 7, no. 1, February 2009, edited by Marlene Laruelle and Sebastien Peyrouse.

Cheng, Nien. *Life and Death in Shanghai*. New York: Grove Press, 1986.

Chi-Ming, Tung. *An Outline History of China*. Hong Kong: Joint Publishing Co., 1982.

China Statistical Yearbook. Published by the National Bureau of Statistics of China 1995–2008.

China–Latin America Task Force. "Findings and Recommendations of the Center for Hemispheric Policy." University of Miami, March–June 2006.

Cohen, Ariel. "The Russia–China Friendship and Co-operation Treaty: A Strategic Shift in Eurasia?" Backgrounder # 1459, Heritage Institute. July 18, 2001.

Committee on IMF Governance Reform, Final Report. IMF, March 24, 2009.

Dowd, Kevin. "Too Big to Fail? Long Term Capital Management and the Federal Reserve." CATO Institute, September 23, 1999.

Driscoll, Edward. "Deflation is not the Problem." CATO Institute, *Australian Financial Review*, June 27, 2003.

Ebrey, Patricia Buckley. *The Cambridge Illustrated History of China*. Cambridge University Press, 1999.

El-Erian, Mohamed. *When Markets Collide: Investment Strategies for the Age of Global Economic Change*. New York: McGraw-Hill, 2008.

Emmott, Bill. *Rivals: How the Power Struggle between China, India and Japan will Shape our Next Decade*. London: Allen Lane, 2008.

Evans, Richard. *Deng Xiaoping and the Making of Modern China*. London: Penguin, 1993.

Fairbank, John M. *China: A New History*. Boston: Harvard University Press, 1992.

Fallowes, James. "Be Nice to the Countries that Lend you Money." *Atlantic Monthly*, January 2009.

Fender, Ingo and Jacob Gyntelberg. "Global Financial Crisis Spurs Unprecedented Policy Actions." Bank of International Settlements, *Quarterly Review*, December 2008.

Finance & Development, IMF, June and December 2008.

Fleckenstein, William A, with Frederick Sheehan. *Greenspan's Bubbles*. New York: McGraw Hill, 2008.

Frankel, Jeffrey. "The Financial and Economic Crisis." Presentation, February 12, 2009.

G20 Finance Ministers' and Central Bank Governors' Communique, March 14, 2009.

G20 London summit—Leaders' Statement, April 2, 2009.

Gang, Yi. Statement by Deputy Governor, People's Bank of China, IMF Eighteenth Meeting, October 11 and 13, 2008.

Gascoigne, Bamber. *The Dynasties of China: a History*. London: Constable & Robinson, 2003.

Garnet, Jacques. *A History of Chinese Civilisation*. Translated by J.R. Foster and Charless Hartman. New York: Cambridge University Press, 1996.

Gieve, Sir John. "Pricing for Perfection." Speech at Bank of England, December 14, 2006.

Gieve, Sir John. "Seven Lessons from the Last Three Years." Speech at Bank of England, February 19, 2009.

Goodman, David S. *China's Regional Development*. London: Routledge for the Royal Institute of International Affairs, 1989.

Green, Malory et al. "China's Trade and Growth: Impact on Selected OECD Countries." OECD Trade Policy Working Paper no. 44, November 28, 2006.

Greenspan, Alan (remarks by). "The Economic Challenges Facing the United States in the New Century." Annual Conference of the National Community Reinvestment Coalition, Washington DC, March 22, 2000.

Greenspan, Alan (remarks by). "The Mortgage Market and Consumer Debt." America's Consumer Bankers Annual Convention, October 19, 2004.

Greenspan, Alan. Testimony before the House Oversight Committee, October 23, 2008.

Haldane, Andrew. "Why Banks Failed the Stress Test." Bank of England, February 13, 2009.

Hansekul, Syetam et al. "China's Markets—A Future Global Force." Deutsche Bank Research, March 2009.

Hessler, Peter. *River Town: Two Years on the Yangtze*. Harper Collins, 2001.

Hoffman, W John, and Michael J Enright (eds). *China into the Future: Making Sense of the World's Most Dynamic Economy*. Singapore: John Wiley & Sons, 2008.

Hunt, Chris. "Financial Turmoil and Global Imbalances: The End of Bretton Woods II?" *Reserve Bank of New Zealand Bulletin* vol. 71, no. 3, September 2008.

Jackson, Richard et al. "China's Long March to Retirement Reform; The Graying of the Middle Kingdom Revisited." Washington DC: Center for Strategic and International Studies and the Prudential Foundation, 2008.

Jaffe, Amy Myers. "Russia and the Caspian States in the Global Energy Balance." Energy Forum, James Baker III Institute for Public Policy, Rice University, May 6, 2009.

Jeanne, Olivier. "International Reserves in Emerging Market Countries: Too much of a good thing?" Brookings Papers in Economic Activity, 2007.

Jenkinson, Nigel. "Risks to the Commercial Property Market and Financial Stability." Bank of England, address to the IPD/IPF Property Investment Conference, Brighton, November 30, 2006.

Kim, Song-Yi, and Louis Kuijs. "Raw Material Prices, Wages and Profitability in China's Industry—How was profitability maintained when input prices and wages increased so fast?" World Bank Research Paper no. 8, October 2007.

Kissinger, Henry. *Diplomacy*. New York: Simon & Schuster, 2004.

Kristof, Nicholas, and WuDunn Shirley. *China Wakes: The Struggle for the Soul of a Rising Power*. New York: Random House, 1994.

Kuhn, Robert. *The Man Who Changed China: The Life and Legacy of Jiang Zemin*. New York: Random House, 2004.

Kumar, Anjali et al. *China's Emerging Capital Markets*. London: FT Publishing, 1997.

Kynge, James. *China Shakes the World: The Rise of a Hungry Nation*. London: Weidenfeld & Nicolson, 2006.

Larner, Robert. *Marco Polo and the Discovery of the World*. New Haven: Yale University Press, 1999.

Li, Cheng. "Hu Jintao's Land Reform: Ambition, Ambiguity and Anxiety." *China Leadership Monitor* no. 27, Hoover Institution. Winter 2009.

Li, Conghua. *The China Consumer Revolution*. Singapore: John Wiley & Sons, 1998.

Liang, Diane Wei. "Spare Me the Lecture." *Prospect Magazine*, June, 2009.

Lieberthal, Kenneth. *Governing China: From Revolution to Reform*. New York: WW Norton, 1995.

Luce, Edward. *In Spite of the Gods: The Strange Rise of Modern India*. London: Little, Brown, 2006.

Magnus, George. *The Age of Aging: How Demographics are Changing the Global Economy and Our World*. Singapore: John Wiley & Sons, 2008.

Menzies, Gavin. *1421 The Year China Discovered America*. London: Harper Perennial, 2004.

Morrison, Wayne M. "China–US Trade Issues." Foreign Affairs, Defense and Trade Division, CRS Issue Brief for Congress, August 4, 2005.

Naughton, Barry. "Understanding the Chinese Stimulus Package." *China Leadership Monitor* no. 28, Hoover Institution. Spring 2009.

Norling, Nicklas. "China and Russia: Partners with Tensions." Policy Perspectives, vol. 4, no. 1 2007.

OECD Economic Statistics 2008.

Pehrson, Christopher J. "String of Pearls: Meeting the Challenge of China's Rising Power across the Asian Littoral." Strategic Studies Institute, United States Army War College, July 2006.

Peyrefitte, Alain. *The Collision of Two Civilisations: Immobile Empire*. Translated by Jon Rothschild. New York: The Harvill Press, 1993.

Recommendation by the Committee of Experts of the President of the General Assembly on Reform of the International Monetary and Financial System. Agenda item 48, 63rd Assembly of the United Nations, March 19, 2009.

Responses to Questions Concerning Long Term Capital Management and Related Events. Letter to Senator Bryan Dorgan and others from the Federal Accounting Office, B-284348, February 23, 2000.

Rogers, Jim. *A Bull in China: Investing Profitably in the World's Greatest Market*. New York: Random House, 2007.

Seagrave, Sterling. *Dragon Lady: The Life and Legend of the Last Empress of China*. New York: Random House, 1992.

Seagrave, Sterling. *The Soong Dynasty*. New York: Harper Collins, 1986.

Shixue, Jiang. "On the Development of Sino–Latin American Relations." Beijing: Chinese Academy of Social Sciences, 2006.

Smith, Adam. *The Theory of Moral Sentiments*. London: Cosimo Classics, 1997.

Smith, Adam. *The Wealth of Nations*. London: Penguin, 1999.

Smith, Sheila. "Japan's New Economic Challenge." Council on Foreign Relations, November 25, 2008.

Snow, Edgar. *Red Star Over China*. London: Random House, 1938.

Snow, John, Treasury Secretary. Testimony before the Senate Committee on Banking, Housing and Urban Affairs, October 30, 2003.

Spence, Jonathan. *The Memory Palace of Matteo Ricci*. New York: Penguin, 1985.

Spence, Jonathan. *The Search for Modern China*. New York: WW Norton, 1990.

Stiglitz, Joseph. *Globalization and its Discontents*. London: Allen Lane, 2002.

Sull, Donald. *Made in China*. Boston: Harvard Business School Press, 2005.

Tam, On Kit. *Financial Reform in China*. London: Routledge, 1995.

Tillman, Hoyt Cleveland. *Confucian Discourse and Chu Hsis's Ascendancy*. Honolulu: University of Hawaii Press, 1992.

US House Banking Committee Hearing, The Growing Balance of Payments Deficits, Washington DC, July 2001.

US Policy toward Latin America in 2009 and Beyond, Hearing before the US House Committee on Foreign Affairs, Washington DC, February 4, 2009.

Winchester, Simon. *The Man who Loved China*. New York: Harper Collins, 2008.

Winchester, Simon. *The River at the Centre of the World*. London: Penguin 1998.

World Bank. "The Chinese Economy: Fighting Inflation, Deepening Reforms." 1996.

World Development Indicators 2009. World Bank.

World Economic Outlook. IMF, January 2009.

Xiaochuan, Zhou. "On Savings." People's Bank of China Web site http://www.pbc.gov.cn. February 2009.

Xiaochuan, Zhou. "Reform the International Monetary System." People's Bank of China Web site http://www.pbc.gov.cn. March 2009.

Xinbo, Wu. "The Promise and Limitations of a Sino–US Partnership." *Washington Quarterly*, Autumn 2004.

Zhisui, Li. *The Private Life of Chairman Mao: The Inside Story of the Man who made Modern China*. New York: Chatto & Windus, 1994.

Index